WHEN TERRORISM AND COUNTERTERRORISM CLASH

WHEN TERRORISM AND COUNTERTERRORISM CLASH

The War on Terror and the Transformation of Terrorist Activity

Ivan Sascha Sheehan

CAMBRIA
PRESS

YOUNGSTOWN, NEW YORK

Library of Congress Cataloging-in-Publication Data

Sheehan, Ivan Sascha.
    When terrorism and counterterrorism clash : the war on terror and the trans-
formation of terrorist activity / Ivan Sascha Sheehan.
        p. cm.
    Includes bibliographical references and index.
    ISBN 978-1-934043-70-7 (alk. paper)
    1. Terrorism. 2. Terrorism—Prevention. 3. War on Terrorism, 2001- I.
Title.

    HV6431.S4686 2007
    363.325—dc22

    2007022024

***To my parents,**
*for their love and encouragement
I am forever grateful*

***To my wife, Kerunne,**
who gives meaning to it all

***And to future generations,**
*in the hope that together we can leave behind
a world less victim to terrorism and violence*

TABLE OF CONTENTS

LIST OF FIGURES

LIST OF TABLES

FOREWORD

The positions of policy commentators often span a spectrum. At one end are positions based on ideology and at the other end are positions based on data and evidence. A given position along this spectrum could be measured by an ideology/evidence index, which is the ratio between accepting a proposition based on its correspondence with one's belief-value system (ideology) versus accepting the proposition based on the results of a systematic, rigorous test of its validity (evidence).

Some policy analysts rely more on ideology than on evidence. In these instances commentators often seek evidence to confirm their cherished ideological views (verification). At the same time, they may turn a blind eye to evidence that would disconfirm their beliefs (falsification). Perhaps never has this been more prevalent than since the atrocities of September 11, 2001, and the Bush administration's response in the form of the global war on terror. At times, an emphasis on ideology has even led to a "rhetoric-reality" disconnect where, for example, President Bush announces "the end of major combat operations in Iraq" with a "Mission Accomplished" banner behind him on the deck of the USS Abraham Lincoln even as combat operations continued.

At the other end of the spectrum are individuals like Dr. Sheehan who seek answers using evidence-based inquiry and research. By merging existing data sets on transnational terrorism and then subjecting them to sophisticated time series analyses, Dr. Sheehan presents the reader with rigorous, empirical, statistical tests of the hypothesis that President George W. Bush's global war on terror has led to a decrease in various indicators of transnational terrorism. He found, with some exceptions, that this is decidedly *not* the case. While these findings may be counterintuitive for some policy makers, his analysis provides new and compelling data that highlights the growing need for evidence-based counterterrorism policy.

Dr. Sheehan's study joins a growing list of commentaries critical of the policies emanating from the White House, but with a significant difference. While many commentators criticize U.S. counterterrorism strategy, their critiques tend to rely on media reports on the worsening sectarian violence in Iraq and on the reconstitution of the Taliban and al Qaeda in Afghanistan. Rigorous testing, using data to analyze the effectiveness of the war on terror, has largely been absent.

In this compelling book, Dr. Sheehan undertakes this task using data and evidence to explore the extent to which the global war on terror has increased or decreased transnational terrorism. This is a study grounded in evidence, not in ideological posturing. It should be noted that Dr. Sheehan does not himself take Mr. Bush to task. He does, however, provide evidence that Mr. Bush's policies have, in the short-term, been counterproductive and self-defeating, enhancing and sustaining the terror it was meant to undermine, thwart, and eliminate.

One significant implication of Dr. Sheehan's counterintuitive findings for the foreign policies of the U.S., Great Britain, Australia, and other countries involved in the war on terrorism is that "winning" the battle against terrorism requires a comprehensive strategy that captures the complexity of the conflict. While military force may be an essential part of such an approach, it cannot be the only part. By merely serving to exacerbate a complex interplay of interdependent causes and conditions, it too often results in further reinforcing the "law of unintended consequences."

Using asymmetric war, social mobilization, and conflict theory, Dr. Sheehan provides readers and policy makers with sophisticated insights that improve our understanding of the potential consequences of current approaches. He also discusses a range of alternative options. These options are intended as complements rather than replacements to a narrow use of "hard power" that tends to target only *symptoms* of complex conflicts among ethnic, national, racial, religious, class, and other groups.

To put it simply, Dr. Sheehan's analysis clearly demonstrates that if we only "fight fire with fire," then the fire may become worse!

As Americans, British, and others contemplate changes in their respective national leaderships in the near future, they may want to consider a shift from policies rooted in ideology towards policies based on evidence. Dr. Sheehan's study makes a forceful case for this "paradigm shift," and for that he deserves our gratitude. This study is a necessary wake-up call that strategic and policy changes are essential if we are to address the problems that give rise to global terrorism in the years ahead.

Dennis J. D. Sandole, Ph.D.
Professor of Conflict Resolution and International Relations
Institute for Conflict Analysis and Resolution (ICAR)
George Mason University

ACKNOWLEDGMENTS

This book is the culmination of a series of events and experiences in my life. No project of this magnitude is completed alone, and I am deeply indebted to a number of individuals for their support and encouragement.

First, I want to thank my mentor at the Institute for Conflict Analysis and Resolution (ICAR) at George Mason University. Professor Dennis Sandole deserves special credit for his support over the years. He encouraged my interest in the study of terrorism when it was still unpopular in academia, and reminded me often that the complexity of conflict requires multiple models, not just one, to understand it in its entirety. In addition, I am grateful to him for his patient reading and rereading of my manuscript and his helpful suggestions throughout the course of this project.

I also want to extend a special note of thanks to Professor Daniel Druckman. I am grateful for his mentorship and the confidence he has placed in me. I likely would not have embarked on a quantitative analysis if it were not for his encouragement and the solid grounding he gave me in research methodology. He taught me to always ask the question, "Where is the evidence?" This book was made better by his sound advice, suggestions, and encouragement.

In addition, I want to thank Professor John Paden. His early enthusiasm for this project was contagious. His comments helped me hone my design, and his vast experience in policy and research was an inspiration to me.

My deepest thanks also go to Dr. Michael Eaddy. His enthusiasm, patience, and encouragement in teaching me, step by step, about time series and helping me with the statistical analyses were invaluable. His guidance was indispensable to this project.

I am also indebted to my friends and colleagues at George Mason University in the field of conflict analysis and resolution and allied fields of study. My conversations with them helped shape my understanding of the dynamics of conflict and terrorism. I look forward to making contributions to the field alongside them for many years to come.

In his address to the Nobel Prize Committee in 1954, Ernest Hemingway remarked that "Writing, at its best, is a lonely life." But it is far less lonely when you have the love and support of your family and close friends.

First and foremost, I am deeply indebted to my parents for their encouragement and unwavering support. Their love, guidance, and tireless commitment have been immeasurable. I will forever be grateful for all they have done for me.

My sister, Tara, is the best sister a brother could ask for. During this project, as with all that I do, she always made me smile, and I am grateful for her love.

Good friends are always a welcome distraction. I especially want to thank my good friends Ryan Stark and Dave Schlossberg for their friendship and support.

Finally, I want to thank the love of my life, my wife and best friend, Kerunne Ketlogetswe. I am more thankful than she will ever know for her companionship. Without her love and encouragement, this book would not have been possible. The completion of this project marks one small achievement in a life of dreams built together.

In writing this book, I tried to follow Joseph Pulitzer's advice on writing: "Put it before them briefly so they will read it, clearly so they will appreciate it, picturesquely so they will remember it, and, above all, accurately so they will be guided by its light." To the extent I have achieved this goal, the individuals mentioned share in this credit.

In a recent interview with *USA Today*, Secretary of State Condoleezza Rice remarked that she was looking forward to going back to Stanford University, where she previously served as Provost, and overseeing academic studies on what went right and wrong in Iraq and the Global War on Terrorism. I hope that this book will be of interest to her and others in the policy community, and I hope that scholars will find it a useful contribution to the study of conflict and terrorism—a contribution that leads to a world less victim to terrorism and violence.

WHEN TERRORISM AND COUNTERTERRORISM CLASH

PART I

A WORLD
OF
TERRORISM
AND
COUNTERTERRORISM

There are very few men—and they are the exceptions—who are able to think and feel beyond the present moment.

—Carl Von Clausewitz

The use of force alone is but temporary. It may subdue for a moment but it does not remove the necessity of subduing again.

—Edmund Burke

CHAPTER 1

THE CHALLENGE
OF GLOBAL TERRORISM

Victory in war is not repetitious, but adapts its form endlessly.
The ability to gain victory by changing and adapting according
to the opponent is called genius.

—Sun Tzu

The 31-year-old Arthur Ashe was a long shot when he walked
onto the court for the Wimbledon final against Jimmy Connors in
1975. Connors, with his driving ground strokes, was clearly the
more powerful player. His aggression had been described as being
like Hemingway's. As one commentator put it, "You see the flash,
then you hear the crack and at last the shell comes." Ashe was
nimble and quick and said to play tennis like chess, but no one
expected him to win. This, after all, was his 11th Wimbledon. In
almost no time, however, Ashe took control and made everything
as difficult as possible for Connors. He was patient. He meditated

between points. He played to the crowd. Then, as Gray described it, he "lobbed, dinked, teased, passed, out-rallied and frustrated the 'odds-on favorite.'"[1] In the end, he beat the reigning champion by focusing on an indirect strategy that completely undercut his opponent's power.

The outcome was not one that was anticipated, but it illustrates a point that is relevant to the study of conflict. Although since Thucydides it has been assumed that power always wins, this is not necessarily the case. The weaker side, as Ivan Arreguin-Toft observes, sometimes does win asymmetric conflicts. In fact, the weaker side has been shown to be victorious in as many as 30% of asymmetric conflicts over a 200-year period. Moreover, weak actors have been increasingly victorious over time.[2]

Today, as the strongest nations of the world combat terrorism from an admittedly weak opponent, that of substate or nonstate terrorists, the lesson from Ashe's match against Connors is an important one. Overwhelming force does not always spell victory in asymmetric conflicts. Sometimes, it has the opposite effect and a weaker adversary, using the right strategy, may score more points rather than fewer and force a stronger actor to back down.[3]

Background. Interstate war dominated the 19th century and the first half of the 20th century. Intrastate or internal war then became a concern after the end of the Cold War. During this period (early to mid- and late 1990s), internal wars accounted for as many as 42 of 49 wars.[4] These wars, however, were becoming increasingly internationalized and in a way that, as Hugo Slim has put it, was "very different from their predecessors during the Cold War when they were internationalized as proxy wars between the two superpower blocs."[5] Of particular concern was the growing role of substate and nonstate actors not subject to international obligations and conducting increasingly more violent activities against foreign targets.

Today, intrastate war is thought to be on the decline.[6] However, terrorism, especially transnational terrorism, broadly defined as politically motivated violence by substate and nonstate actors against foreign targets,[7] is now dictating much of the political and security agendas of the world's countries. Despite the political and security importance of this phenomenon, especially since the September 11, 2001, attacks on the World Trade Center and the Pentagon, terrorism until recently was, in Senechal de la Roche's words, understudied and "greatly undertheorized."[8] More important for this book, relatively little research has been paid to the dynamics and outcomes of conflicts when terrorism and counterterrorism clash.

This may be because compared with interstate and intrastate wars, transnational terrorism causes relatively few deaths.[9] It may also be because for years terrorism was considered too "policy oriented" an area of research in academia and was, therefore, only a subject of short-term episodic interest among scholars.[10] In addition, as Rubenstein points out, it may be because, even before September 11 but especially since that time, there has been a tendency to minimize the rational instrumental aspects of terrorism in favor of an emphasis on its expressive purposes.[11]

Much of the quantitative work on terrorism has focused on relatively static economic and political background conditions that might be relevant to the causes of terrorism. Although there is empirical evidence supporting the causal role of some of these variables (modernization, gross domestic product, political repression, lack of education), the results are fragile.[12] In other words, theory is limited. At the same time, although there is a growing qualitative literature on the dynamics of terrorist violence, there has been little systematic work.[13] In particular, relatively little research attention has been paid to the ways in which the strategies of governments and those of adversaries who use terrorism for their own objectives shape some outcomes rather than others.

THE PROBLEM

The relationship between the use of preemptive force, as a strategy of government, and subsequent terrorist activity, especially transnational terrorist activity, is a matter of considerable importance in the context of the current and ongoing military effort known as the Global War on Terrorism or, more briefly, the GWOT.[14] From the Cold War through the 1990s, U.S. security policy was based largely on strategies of containment and deterrence. Although force in the form of preemptive military strikes was used after attacks on U.S. interests in the 1990s, such strikes were only used episodically and were not at the center of U.S. security policy. Moreover, they were conducted largely as tactics within the larger strategy of containment and deterrence.[15] In this environment, transnational terrorism, as a form of calculated politically motivated violence mounted by substate actors on U.S. or other foreign targets, was a relatively low-level security concern.

This situation changed with the September 11, 2001, attacks by al Qaeda on New York's World Trade Center and the Pentagon in Arlington, Virginia. In the aftermath of September 11, transnational terrorism moved to the center of U.S. foreign policy, and in a departure from the strategy of deterrence, the Bush administration began to articulate a new strategy of preemptive force in reference to the threat of what it called "global terrorism" or "terrorism of global reach." A basic assumption behind this shift in strategy was the notion that terrorist operatives and resources needed to be taken out, *preemptively*, before they could mount attacks.[16]

Within days of September 11, President Bush declared a "Global War on Terrorism" and called on the world's countries to join him. Within a month of 9/11, he led a coalition of troops to Afghanistan with the express intention of hunting down al Qaeda operatives, taking out their training camps, and toppling the Taliban regime that supported them. Subsequently, and on the basis that Iraq had weapons of mass destruction or otherwise posed a potential terrorist threat, the Bush administration, together with a smaller coalition of countries, proceeded to invade Iraq to remove the regime of Saddam Hussein.

The effectiveness of these military actions and the preemptive strategy underlying them are matters of considerable debate. As the U.S. presidential elections approached in 2004, the Bush administration congratulated itself on the capture of Saddam Hussein, and it claimed that as a result of the wars in Afghanistan and Iraq (both articulated as part of the GWOT), al Qaeda had lost its sanctuary, that three fourths of its leadership were captured or killed, that the remnants were now on the run, and that the ability of this group and its associated and affiliated organizations to conduct terrorism had been severely limited. Nonetheless, it was struggling with evidence, based on photos released in April 2004, of U.S. abuse of Iraqi prisoners at Abu Ghraib. In this climate, scholars such as Lake (2002) argued that the new strategy of preemptive force was an "overreaction" and precisely the kind of overreaction the perpetrators of 9/11 aimed to provoke.[17] According to this view, the Bush administration's strategy of force had inflamed moderates in the Muslim world and increased al Qaeda's recruiting power and operational capacity.[18] As a result, al Qaeda had only "morphed" into a looser organization with greater support and more offshoots and associated organizations, which were now engaged in more terrorist activity than ever before.

QUESTIONS

Has the GWOT, with its underlying strategy of preemptive force, decreased transnational terrorist activity, or has it had the reverse effect and widened this threat? And to what extent have associated events, including the invasion of Iraq, the capture of Iraq's former dictator, Saddam Hussein, and evidence, after Abu Ghraib, of U.S. soldiers abusing Iraqi detainees, affected this dynamic?

Given the enormous resources in blood and treasure that the United States has spent on the War on Terrorism, these questions have implications for U.S. foreign policy. Insofar as clashes between those who engage in global or transnational terrorism and those who seek to thwart this phenomenon represent an emerging form of conflict, these questions also have implications for conflict theory.

COMPETING THEORIES

Della Porta observes that scholars of collective action have long argued that when governments respond to oppositional violence with tactics that are "more tolerant, selective, and softer," the likelihood of subsequent violence increases. On the other hand, when regimes carry out measures that are highly forceful, diffuse, and "harder," challengers are expected to have difficulty mobilizing further action.[19] Taken to the extreme, this means, in Ralph Peter's (2004, p. 26) words: "There is no substitute for shedding the enemy's blood."

The benefits of such an approach, however, have not been conclusively demonstrated.[20] Ethan Bueno de Mesquita points out that governments engage in forceful offensive measures ("crackdowns") to *prevent* terrorist attacks in the future.[21] But such measures can have mixed effects. They may decrease the ability of existing terrorists and their organizations to mount effective actions. However, they can also lead to displacement of attacks or substitution of new means of attacks.[22] In addition, as Lichbach points out, offensive measures can drive a hard core further underground where they become more organized, dedicated, and deadly.[23] Moreover, such "hard tactics," if not highly selective, may be perceived as arbitrary and unjust, creating anger and frustration in a wider population.[24] This effect, as Lichbach citing Greene observes, can "lower the government's legitimacy and raise the society's revolutionary potential."[25]

When does force escalate terrorist activity? When does it have a deescalating effect? In "Why Big Nations Lose Small Wars," Andrew Mack argues that the key variable in asymmetric conflicts is resolve or will.[26] According to this logic, big nations lose small wars, including those against guerillas and terrorists, when their will falters or, as Colonel Ralph Peters put it in an interview in 2003, they are seen as "weak-willed."[27] This line of argument is consistent with rational choice models that posit that rational actors will back down or shift into lower-level violence in the face of superior force or signaling of force.[28]

Others have proposed that what is critical in such conflicts is "strategic interaction." In his analysis of more than 200 asymmetric conflicts, Arreguin-Toft found that when strong actors used direct approaches (e.g., attrition and blitzkrieg) and weak actors used the same approach, strong actors almost always prevailed. However, when weak actors employed indirect approaches (guerilla war and terrorism) against direct attacks, they were usually able to sustain and escalate their activities. He attributed this result to the fact that in such interactions strong actors almost always became impatient and resorted to barbarism; that is, violation of the laws of war, and this outcome had an inflaming effect.[29]

Lake has suggested that such an overreaction is precisely what terrorists and other insurgents want to provoke—to radicalize moderates and gain support. Taking a resource-mobilization model (which is consistent with Arreguin-Toft's model but departs from the strict rational choice bargaining paradigm), he argues that terrorists resort to violence not because of misinformation or miscalculation of adversaries' resources, will, or power, or even because of fundamental issues they want to bargain, but because "no bargain is acceptable to them under the current distribution of capabilities." Terrorism, in this analysis, is undertaken to provoke a massive response and is specifically designed to "shift the balance of power between the parties" and build support, perhaps "to produce a better bargain at some point in the distant future."[30]

Insights from conflict resolution theory support the contention that escalation in conflicts is highest when hard tactics have a mobilizing effect. Early on in their work on "conflict spirals," Dean Pruitt and Jeffrey Rubin showed that conflict tends to escalate when tactics move from light to heavy, issues proliferate, more and more parties join, and there is a shift from doing well to winning and hurting the other.[31] Later, Rubin, Pruitt, and Kim proposed that the escalatory effect of heavy tactics was largely mediated by the psychological states they produced in the other party. In particular, they proposed that when such tactics produced anger, blame, fear, and threats to image, the potential for escalation was highest and was most likely to produce polarization.[32]

Extended to the problem of terrorism, these considerations suggest that the use of massive force is unlikely to have had the desired effect of deescalating terrorist activity and more likely to have had the reverse effect. Still, the "big picture," as former Secretary of Defense Donald Rumsfeld has put it, is not yet clear and the "complexity of conflict," as Dennis Sandole has described it, is such that reality does not always fit neatly into present theories or paradigms.[33]

PRIOR RESEARCH

So far, to the author's knowledge, only one systematic quantitative study has attempted to analyze the impact of 9/11 and the military effort known as the War on Terrorism on subsequent transnational terrorism. That study conducted by Enders and Sandler (2005) focuses on changes in quarterly transnational terrorist activity using the ITERATE database compiled by Edward Mickolus. However, since it makes an operative assumption that terrorist activity is cyclical, it does not specifically test the extent to which transnational terrorism has escalated. Moreover, it does not try to separate out the impact of the War on Terrorism on the chief target of that war; that is, al Qaeda and its shadowy network of affiliated Islamist terrorist organizations and associations. In addition, the analysis uses a pre-intervention period extending back to 1968 (although one could argue that such a lengthy period may dilute significant changes in transnational terrorism that occurred in the 1990s), and the analysis only extends through the second quarter of 2003. As a result, even if it had attempted to test if escalation had occurred, it would not have been able to capture the potentially inflaming effects of such events as the capture of Saddam Hussein in December 2003 and the release of photos from Abu Ghraib in April 2004.

GOALS

This time series intervention analysis[34] of quarterly transnational terrorist events after the onset of the War on Terrorism seeks to contribute to the debate in several ways.

First, to capture more data and provide a richer picture of the effects, the analysis uses transnational terrorist event data from more than one transnational terrorism incident data set (ITERATE plus RAND–MIPT).[35]

Second, the analysis specifically tests the force escalation hypothesis; that is, the extent to which the GWOT, with its emphasis on military force, has increased transnational terrorism.

Third, the analysis extends through December 2004. As a result, in addition to examining the effects of the invasions of Afghanistan in late 2001 and Iraq in March 2003, it looks at the inflaming effects of the capture of Saddam Hussein in December 2003 and the release of photos of alleged prisoner abuse from Abu Ghraib in April 2004.

Fourth, to further test the escalation hypothesis, I use *new variables* to measure potential escalation in transnational terrorist activity. In addition to examining moving averages of quarterly counts of incidents and of lethal incidents, I examine averages of quarterly days of transnational terrorist activity to see if there has been an increase in the number of operative days of transnational terrorist activity. This measure may be important since those who engage in terrorism seek publicity and the number of operative days may be a good proxy for media coverage. (The assumption here is that when terrorist incidents are mounted on more days, they are more likely to be covered more days in the media.) Also, on the basis that escalation implies a widening of activity, I examine if attacks are more dispersed; that is, if they occur in more places (countries) and if the percentage share of incidents in the Middle East and in predominantly Muslim countries is increased.

Fifth, on the basis that escalation could be seen to mean a widening of a conflict in terms of the targets, I examine whether there has been a change in the makeup of victims of attacks. Specifically, I test the extent to which victims of transnational terrorist attacks, since the onset of the War on Terrorism, are more likely to be multinational (i.e., include more than one nationality or to be members of multinational companies or multinational organizations such as the United Nations or international nongovernmental organizations).[36]

Finally, I provide comparisons between the ITERATE and RAND databases and between unique and overlapping incidents in the data sets. These comparisons are designed to shed light on the composition of each database and may be helpful in future research.

SIGNIFICANCE

The study presented here extends Asymmetric War and Conflict Resolution theories to transnational terrorism. Using transnational terrorism events data, it tests contending theories about the effects of force on this phenomenon. More specifically, it tests the extent to which preemptive force, in general, and the War on Terrorism, in particular, have had an escalating effect on transnational terrorism. As such, the study has important theoretical, empirical, and policy implications.

OUTLINE

Chapter 2 presents the background, rationale for, and controversies over the preemptive military strategy known as the GWOT. Chapters 3 and 4 examine the conceptual and theoretical issues related to defining and explaining terrorism and counterterrorism, and chapter 4 also provides a synopsis of previous research on the effects of force as a response to terrorism as a tactic of contention.

Chapter 5 introduces the main hypotheses, the design of the study, and the rationale for merging two database sources (ITERATE and RAND–MIPT) for the analysis. This chapter also discusses the time series statistical techniques that are employed to test change in transnational terrorist activity and the limitations of the potential findings.

Chapter 6 contains the results of my study. In this chapter, I describe the overall characteristics of the merged data set. I then present the results of the time series analyses of the impact of the onset of the GWOT and the other events (the invasion of Iraq, the capture of Saddam Hussein, and the release of photos from Abu Ghraib) on the frequency, dispersion, lethality, type of attack, and type of victim of subsequent transnational terrorist activity. In this chapter, I also provide comparisons of the transnational terrorist data in ITERATE and RAND, and I discuss and provide comparisons of overlapping and unique incidents. These comparisons and the discussion are presented to shed more light on the sources of the data used in the time series analysis.

In chapter 7, I discuss the theoretical and policy implications of the research for the future of the GWOT.

CHAPTER 2

STRATEGIC CHOICES

GRAND STRATEGY

Deterrence: A Cold War Strategy

During the Cold War, the United States adopted a foreign policy based on deterrence. Although many definitions of this policy exist, deterrence was almost always defined in terms of a coercive threat. As Thomas Schelling observed in 1966, deterrence is about intentions.[1] It is, in Patrick Morgan's words, "the use of threats of harm to prevent someone from doing something you do not want him to."[2] It can be argued that deterrence made sense in the context of the Cold War in which either one of two powers (the United States and the USSR) had the capacity to annihilate the other. After the end of the Cold War and the fall of the USSR, deterrence continued to be used by the United States and other countries, especially Israel, to combat national separatist movements thought to be a threat to local or regional security. Israeli analyst Yehoshaphat Harkabi defined deterrence as the "threat of heavy punishment for an act by the enemy in order to persuade him to desist from that act."[3]

A critical aspect of deterrence was that it had to work. As Zeev Maoz put it, deterrence is

> A policy through which one attempts to scare off a would-be attacker by holding out a drawn sword. It works as long as the sword is not being used. When the sword becomes covered with blood, deterrence is said to have failed, no matter whose blood was spilled.[4]

In the United States, references to deterrence continued to be common in the military and policy communities as late as 1997. However, after the 9/11 attacks, President Bush ordered the Department of Defense to build a new strategy to address the increasingly deadly terrorist threat. In response to this directive, the Department of Defense assembled the National Defense University Task Force on Combating Terrorism. The task force proposed a "3-D" approach that had three principal goals: to defeat, deter, and diminish the enemy.[5] However, as Doron Almog observes, by the time the strategy was adopted, the word "deter" had been replaced with two others—"deny" and "defend."[6] The final document, issued in February 2003, thus put forth a "4D strategy" that rested on four pillars—to defeat, deny, diminish, and defend against the adversary.[7]

Armed with this new statement of purpose, the United States effectively abandoned the doctrine of classical deterrence that some believed became irrelevant with the 1991 collapse of the Soviet Union. The new doctrine made it clear that force would now be central to achieving U.S. objectives no matter how long these objectives took to accomplish:

> There will be no quick or easy end to this conflict. ...Ours is a strategy of direct and continuous action against terrorist

groups, the cumulative effect of which will initially disrupt, over time degrade, and ultimately destroy the terrorist organizations. The more frequently and relentlessly we strike the terrorists across all fronts, using all the tools of statecraft, the more effective we will be.[8]

After 9/11: Preemption and Preventive War

The concept of preemption—and, every bit as importantly, preventive war—had already been introduced in the Bush Administration's 2002 *National Security Strategy*, which asserted that

> The United States has long maintained the option of preemptive actions to counter a sufficient threat to our national security, and "the United States will, if necessary, act preemptively."[9]

President Bush had addressed preemption in a major policy address at the U.S. Military Academy 3 months earlier on June 1, 2002. In this address, he stated, "If we wait for threats to materialize, we will have waited too long," and he declared that "our security will require all Americans…to be ready for preemptive action when necessary to defend our liberty and defend our lives."[10]

On June 6, 2002, the concept of preemption was further emphasized in a talk given by Vice President Richard Cheney, who, in a meeting with the National Association of Home Builders, declared, "Wars are not won on the defensive. We must take the battle to the enemy and, where necessary, preempt grave threats to our country before they materialize."[11]

At this time, the United States and coalition forces had already dispatched most of the remnants of al Qaeda in Afghanistan and were involved in replacing the now weakened Taliban regime with a new government led by Hamid Karzai. The remarks of the president and vice president, however, foreshadowed the run-up to the Iraq war. This became more apparent by the close of the summer of 2002.

By August of 2002, Secretary of Defense Donald Rumsfeld, in an interview with *Fox News*, indicated that the United States could not wait for proof that Saddam had weapons of mass destruction. He then compared the prelude to war against Iraq with the prelude to World War II, when the Allies appeased Hitler, and he rejected alternative points of view other than war, saying

> The people who argue [against invading Iraq] have to ask themselves how they're going to feel at that point where another event occurs and it's not a conventional event, but it's an unconventional event.[12]

Within a month, National Security Advisor Condoleezza Rice was elaborating on the security strategy using a graphic analogy to convey the increased risk of waiting and the rationale for preemption: "We don't want the smoking gun to become a mushroom cloud."[13]

THE STRATEGY DEBATE

Not surprisingly, the shift toward a policy of preemptive force met with considerable debate. Ethicists weighed in almost as soon as the policy was formulated. On September 23, 2002, 100 scholars made a one-sentence statement in the *Chronicle of Higher Education*: "As Christian ethicists, we share a common moral presumption against a preemptive war on Iraq by the United States."[14] In October 2002 Paul Schroeder set forth the ethical case against the war in Iraq in an article in the *American Conservative*:

> A more dangerous, illegitimate norm and example can hardly be imagined. As could easily be shown by history, it completely subverts previous standards for judging the legitimacy of resorts to war, justifying any number of wars hitherto considered unjust and aggressive. It would, for example, justify not only the Austro-German decision

for preventive war on Serbia in 1914, condemned by most historians, but also a German attack on Russia and/or France as urged by some German generals on numerous occasions between 1888 and 1914. It would in fact justify almost any attack by any state on any other for almost any reason. This is not a theoretical or academic point. The American example and standard for preemptive war, if carried out, would invite imitation and emulation, and get it. One can easily imagine plausible scenarios in which India could justly attack Pakistan or vice versa, or Israel any one of its neighbours, or China Taiwan, or South Korea North Korea, under this rule that suspicion of what a hostile regime might do justifies launching preventive wars to overthrow it.[15]

Some military analysts applauded the new approach. "We have cast off old, failed rules of warfare" for a new paradigm "that makes previous models of warfare obsolete," wrote military analyst Colonel Ralph Peters.[16] Others challenged this position. "Adopting preemptive strikes (followed by bombing more massive than anything since World War II)," declared Colonel John Brinsfield, a former professor at the Army War College,

Should never be a normative part of our ethical thinking about war. To embrace preemptive strikes as normal policy rather than a very narrowly defined exception to the rules of civilized warfare is not to advance to a position of "waging just wars humanely" (quoting Peters) but rather to retreat to barbarism, waging war whenever we think "might makes right."[17]

U.S. foreign policy analysts were divided. Neoconservatives, such as Irving Kristol and Charles Krauthammer, approved the policy as a means of protecting the United States and at the same time bringing needed reforms to other parts of the world. But as early as August 2002, in an opinion piece published in *The Wall Street Journal*, Brent Scowcroft, national security advisor to the former President Bush, warned that "an attack on Iraq at this time would seriously jeopardize, if not destroy, the global counterterrorist campaign we have undertaken." Similarly, in an article in *The Washington Post*, former Secretary of State Henry Kissinger said that "military intervention should be attempted only if we are willing to sustain such an effort for however long it is needed."[18]

In the academic world, classical realists such as Robert Jervis, John Robert Mearsheimer, and Stephen Walt raised questions about the consequences of moving away from policies of containment and deterrence that had worked in the past and that, they felt, had more promise for the current situation.[19] Today, some of these experts fear that their concerns have become a reality. In a panel discussion at the Fletcher School, for example, Walt recently remarked that "the U.S. is now regarded with greater fear and suspicion, than any other time in our history," a development that has encouraged other states to begin to balance against us. Citing a 19th-century practitioner of realism, he went on to recall Prussian leader Otto von Bismarck's observation that "preventive war is committing suicide for fear of death."[20]

Other foreign policy analysts came to different conclusions. For example, one of America's leading scholars of foreign policy, Yale's John Lewis Gaddis, was cautiously optimistic. Citing the Bush plan as the "most sweeping shift in U.S. grand strategy since the beginning of the Cold War," he argued that much depended on how the world responded to it. Contrary to the conventional wisdom, he also argued that the current strategy of preemption was not really a radical departure and that the United States has responded with preemption at other times in its history when it was vulnerable. He called attention in particular to the British burning of Washington in 1814. In response to that attack, Gaddis recounts, John Quincy Adams, then secretary of state to James Monroe, developed a strategy of preemptive action in relation to the North

American continent as a way of preventing nonstate actors who, with or without state support, might gain footholds from which they could threaten the United States. Gaddis argues that Adams' "grand strategy" remained in effect throughout most of the 19th and 20th centuries and was only abandoned after World War II when the United States had a monopoly on nuclear weapons and the USSR became its new adversary. In his opinion, we have returned to a situation that is similar to that which 19th-century strategists had to contend with.[21]

CALCULATING THE COSTS

> Wars are costly undertakings.
>
> —William Hartung

Monetary Costs

In the first year alone, the direct costs to the United States of Operation Enduring Freedom, that is, the war in Afghanistan, are estimated to have been from $15 to $20 billion.[22] The costs to the United States of Operation Iraqi Freedom for the first 21 months (through December 2004) are estimated to have been as high as $128 billion. That does not include major maintenance, the replacement of destroyed equipment, and costs associated with the need to recruit more troops and retrain those deployed to Iraq. Through 2005, Anthony Cordesman estimates that the cost of military operations in the Iraq theater will be between $212 and $232 billion. By the end of 2007, he indicates they could be as high as $316 billion.[23] In defense of these costs, some observers have pointed out that, by historical standards, the United States is now devoting a smaller proportion (4%) of its gross national product to defense than in the Reagan years.[24] However, others have noted that with budget requests made in early 2005, the costs of the military operations in Iraq and Afghanistan and other efforts since the September 11, 2001, attacks have surged to $277 billion, a figure that "exceeds the inflation-adjusted $200 billion cost of World War I and is approaching the $350 billion cost of the Korean War." The extent of these costs is increasingly raising concerns about the U.S. deficit, which reached as high as $412 billion in 2004.[25]

Costs in Lives

The United States, however, was not just spending its financial treasure. The war in Iraq was also costing lives. By the end of 2004, more than 1,300 members of the U.S. military had died in the war in Iraq.[26] Moreover, an independent organization, Iraq Body Count, estimated that between 14,284 and 16,419 Iraqi civilians had perished as a result of violence in the 18 months after the invasion.[27] Other estimates, based on household surveys by Johns Hopkins and Columbia University researchers working with Baghdad's Al-Mustansiriya University, put the excess Iraqi death toll as high as 98,000 in the same time period.[28]

Costs in Public Opinion

The wars in Afghanistan and Iraq were also becoming more costly in terms of public opinion. In October 2003, Carl Conetta pointed out that public opinion and, in particular, opinion in the Arab and Muslim world was at a 25-year low, making it difficult to build the cooperation necessary to fight terrorism.[29]

On May 1, 2003, President Bush had declared an end to major combat operations in Iraq, and he also declared "one victory in the war on terror that began on 9/11."[30] In a similar vein, Cofer Black, the Department of State's counterterrorism coordinator, stated that now al Qaeda would have to "put up or shut up. They had failed. It proves the Global War on Terrorism is effective."[31] Within weeks, however, suicide attacks in Saudi Arabia, Morocco, Israel, and

Chechnya suggested a very different conclusion. Although White House claims that a new spate of insurgent attacks in Iraq only showed how "desperate" the adversary had become, the effectiveness and purpose of these measures was increasingly being called into question.

> Wars begin when you want but don't end when you wish.
> —Niccolo Machiavelli

In September 2003, almost 2 years after the removal of the Taliban in Afghanistan and 4 months after the fall of the Iraqi regime, London's International Institute for Strategic Studies (IISS) issued a report concluding that, notwithstanding al Qaeda's loss of its infrastructure in Afghanistan and the killing or capture of perhaps one third of its leadership, al Qaeda is "now reconstituted and doing business in a somewhat different manner, but more insidious and just as dangerous as in its pre-September 11 incarnation." In addition, it suggested that the West's "counterterrorism effort had perversely impelled an already highly decentralized and elusive transnational terrorist network to become even harder to identify and neutralize." Among other things, the destruction of its camps in Afghanistan meant that al Qaeda "no longer concentrated its forces in clusters discernible and targetable from the air," which in turn meant that the "lion's share of the counterterrorism burden rested on law enforcement and intelligence agencies."[32]

The end of 2003 saw the capture of Saddam Hussein and, although this event was proclaimed a victory by the U.S. administration, there was little reason for optimism. In late 2003, the U.S.-based Center for Strategic and International Studies (CSIS) had reported that al Qaeda was training in the Russian Republic of Chechnya and had new ties in South America.[33] In the first 6 months of 2004, CSIS found that Islamist militancy and terrorism were spreading in Indonesia and in Central Asia, and it indicated that the March 11 bombings in Madrid showed a new level of sophistication.[34] CSIS also reported that al Qaeda had new operational bases in at least six countries including Kenya, Sudan, Pakistan, and Chechnya,[35] and the similarities between suicide bombings in predominantly Muslim Chechnya and Riyadh, Saudi Arabia, led Vladmir Putin of Russia to conclude that they were conducted by the same organization.[36]

For the United States in the early part of 2004, the need for better intelligence became increasingly more urgent. This may explain why some soldiers and interrogators began to turn to more aggressive methods. In April 2004 allegations of torture and abuse of Iraqi detainees by U.S. soldiers at Iraq's Abu Ghraib prison began to emerge, and for much of the rest of the spring and summer, what came to be known as the "Abu Ghraib prison scandal" dominated international headlines. Although the U.S. administration tried to play down the extent of torture and abuse, the release of photos showing the use of hoods, dogs, leashes, and sexual humiliation at Abu Ghraib rapidly became recruiting tools for opposition groups.

In May 2004 IISS declared that despite its post–September 11 losses, al Qaeda still had more than 18,000 potential terrorists operating in as many as 60 countries. During this period, the "postwar" Iraqi resistance was thought to be growing, from about 5,000 hardened fighters in mid-2003 to over 20,000 including as many as 1,000 foreign Islamic fighters who had infiltrated Iraqi territory.[37] By June, CSIS concluded that the U.S. government claim in early 2004 that two thirds of the al Qaeda leadership had been eliminated "now seems like poor consolation as a new generation of terrorists is emerging in Iraq and around the globe."[38] For many, the catalyst was Abu Ghraib. However, interviews of foreign fighters later caught in Iraq indicated that images of abuse at the detention center at Guantanamo Bay also inspired a willingness to fight.[39]

By late 2004, there was a growing perception that the Iraqi insurgency was becoming, in the words of U.S. Central Command Lieutenant General Lance Smith, "more effective: they may use doorbells today to blow things up. They may use remote controls from toys tomorrow. And as we adapt, they adapt."[40] In July CSIS had reported evidence that Osama bin Laden was now focusing his efforts on Nigeria and West Africa. There was also evidence of renewed enthusiasm for al Qaeda in Yemen, where cooperation with the United States in the War on Terror had incited Muslim radicals, and in the summer of 2004, Abu Hafs al-Masri Brigade was known to have posted an announcement making reference to their desire to turn Yemen into another battleground for U.S. forces:

> Our goals in the next phase: expanding the circle of conflict by spreading operations all around the world. (We will) drag America into a third swamp—after Iraq and Afghanistan—and let it be Yemen, God willing.[41]

For some, the "clash of civilizations" envisaged as early as 1993 by Harvard's Samuel P. Huntington appeared to be becoming a reality.[42] By mid-2004, Brookings scholar P.W. Singer observed that

> While the United States and its allies have seized a portion of al Qaeda lieutenants and assets, the organization remains vibrant, its senior leadership is largely intact, its popularity greater than ever, its ability to recruit unbroken, and its ideology and funds spreading across a global network present in places ranging from Algeria and Belgium to Indonesia and Iraq. Of greatest concern, its potential to strike at American citizens and interests both at home and abroad continues.[43]

Singer went on to express concern that "at a broader level, the United States and the wider Islamic world stand at a point of historic and dangerous crisis."[44] There was no question that support for the United States had decreased in the Arab world. As early as June 2003, a Pew survey of individuals in Muslim countries found that favorable opinions of the United States were present in only 4% of the population in Saudi Arabia, in 6% in Morocco and Jordan, and in 13% in Egypt. Similar patterns held across the rest of the Muslim world, from Indonesia to Pakistan.[45] A year after the invasion of Iraq, Pew polls indicated that anger toward the United States was still pervasive in Muslim countries and opposition to the war almost universal. Moreover, Osama bin Laden was viewed favorably by large percentages in Pakistan (65%), Jordan (55%), and Morocco (45%). [46]

Perhaps most important, what the United States had described as a preemptive "war on terrorism" was becoming broadly interpreted as "a war on Islam." As a result, Singer claimed, "relations between the world's dominant state power and the world's community of over 1.4 billion Muslim believers stand at question." [47]

DECISIONS WITHOUT DATA?

Still, the big picture was not clear. As indicated in an October 2003 memo, even U.S. Secretary of Defense Donald Rumsfeld had questions:

> Today, we lack metrics to know if we are winning or losing the global war on terror. Are we capturing, killing, or deterring and dissuading more terrorists every day than the *madrassas* and the radical clerics are recruiting, training, and deploying against us?
>
> Does the U.S. need to fashion a broad, integrated plan to stop the next generation of terrorists? The U.S. is putting relatively little effort into a long-range plan, but we are putting a great deal of effort into trying to stop terrorists. The cost-benefit ratio is against us! Our cost is billions against

the terrorists' costs of millions.... . Is our current situation such that "the harder we work, the behinder we get"?[48]

Some observers took these questions to mean that the administration was making decisions without adequate data. Princeton economist Alan Krueger and Stanford political scientist David Laitin, for example, declared that

> The statement was a stinging acknowledgment that the government lacks both classified and unclassified data to make critical policy decisions. It is also a reminder that only accurate information, presented without political spin, can help the public and decision-makers know where the United States stands in the war on terrorism and how best to fight it.[49]

Jeffrey Record of the Center for International Strategy, Technology and Policy (CISTP) observes that traditional wars provided "clear standards of measuring success in the form of territory gained and enemy forces destroyed or otherwise removed from combat." He argues that these standards, however, were always of "limited utility against irregular enemies that fought to different standards of success, and they are of almost no use in gauging success against a terrorist threat like al Qaeda."[50] As he points out, citing Bruce Hoffman, terrorists "do not function in the open as armed units, generally do not attempt to seize or hold territory, deliberately avoid engaging enemy military forces in combat and rarely exercise any direct control or sovereignty over either territory or population."[51] Moreover, "al Qaeda has demonstrated impressive regenerative powers," in part because, as Daniel Byman points out, it is

> not just a distinct terrorist organization: it is a movement that seeks to inspire and coordinate other groups and individuals.

> Even if al Qaeda is taking losses beyond its ability to recuperate, there is still a much broader Islamist movement that is hostile to the United States, seeks to overthrow U.S. allies and is committed to mass casualty terrorist violence... . The conceptual key is this: al Qaeda is not a single terrorist group but a global insurgency.[52]

Record concludes that against such an enemy, "tallies of dead and captured are problematic," although the capture of al Qaeda leaders may contribute to success by "removing dangerous operatives from circulation and providing new sources of intelligence on al Qaeda."[53]

DEMANDS FOR ACCOUNTABILITY

Nonetheless, by the end of 2004, there was an increasing demand for accountability and measurement of results. The problem of accountability became a special focus in January when, in a confirmation hearing for Secretary of State, National Security Advisor Dr. Condoleeza Rice was asked to comment specifically on this matter by Senator Feingold:

> I'd like to have you say a little bit about how do we measure success—not a list of things we've done, but how do we measure how well the terrorists are doing? How do we know whether they're picking up steam in terms of picking up recruits and gathering more help around the world or not? How do we measure this thing?[54]

Condoleeza Rice, who was confirmed but with senators objecting, made it clear that our ability to measure "this thing" is imperfect. She added,

> One of the hardest things about this is this is a very shadowy network whose numbers are hard to count. It's important and difficult to know what is a hard-core terrorist who's committed to the jihad and would never be reformable

in any way versus somebody who might just be attracted
to the philosophy because they're jobless or hopeless, or
whatever, and might be brought back into the fold. That's
the kind of important question for which we, frankly, don't
have a measurement, and I don't think we're going to. I
think we're going to see this in broader strokes.[55]

The issue of measurement became, if possible, more heated in
April 2005 when the State Department discovered that the number of international terrorist incidents had increased in 2004 and
announced that it was stripping its congressionally mandated
Annual Report on Terrorism of all terrorism-related statistics for
that year.[56] The previous April, the State Department retracted
its annual report because it understated the number of incidents
for 2003. This new move met with considerable criticism. In particular, there was "concern that the move was designed to shield
the government from questions about the success of its effort to
combat terrorism by eliminating what amounted to the only year-
to-year benchmark of progress." Within days, the administration
did release the data through the National Counterterrorism Center
(NCTC) but urged reporters not to compare the numbers for 2004
with those for earlier years because, it claimed, the criteria for
counting had changed.[57] This recommendation also met with considerable criticism. "Inevitably there are some judgment calls that
go into deciding what is a terrorist event," said Princeton economist Alan Krueger, "but it is astonishing to me that three years into
the 'war on terrorism' there is not more interest by the administration in keeping track of terrorist incidents." Others voiced concern about the implications of the State Department abandoning
its report. "How can we hold ourselves accountable for achieving
benchmarks of progress in this struggle," asked Senator Russell
Feingold (D-Wis.), "if we have no clear idea of what exactly it is
that would constitute success?"[58]

CHAPTER 3

THE NATURE OF TERRORISM AND COUNTERTERRORISM

WHAT IS TERRORISM?

Defining the target of the War on Terrorism poses immediate difficulties. Although *terrorism* is thought to be as old as history, there is no one definition of the term.[1] As Charles Tilly has aptly stated, the definition "sprawls across a wide range of human cruelties."[2] The term *terrorism* first entered the Western vocabulary in relation to state-organized violence and repression and, in particular, to describe the actions of French revolutionaries against their domestic enemies in 1793 and 1794. During what became known as the Reign of Terror, France's new government legally executed as many as 17,000 people, and it is estimated that another 23,000 people were illegally executed. In subsequent years, *terrorism* was used to refer to the actions of dictators such as Stalin, Hitler, and

Pol Pot, but it was also expanded to include attacks by nongovernment entities, such as the Irish Republican Army (IRA), Basque separatists, and the Palestinian Liberation Organization (PLO), on governments and the public at large.[3]

Today, multiple definitions of terrorism exist. Alex Schmid and Albert Jongman have counted as many as 109 different ones.[4] Terrorism expert Walter Laqueur has also counted over 100 definitions and has come to the conclusion that the "only general characteristic generally agreed on is that terrorism involves violence and the threat of violence."[5]

Ideally, conceptualizations of phenomena should avoid the inclusion of irrelevant attributes, and they should also avoid the exclusion of relevant attributes. In addition, they should have a clear conceptual logic, and empirical measures derived from them should be valid, reliable, and replicable.[6] Unfortunately, much of the literature on terrorism employs conceptualizations that are, in the words of Monty Marshall, "too broad to be analytically useful, too narrow to be analytically meaningful, or too detailed or too complex to be applied systematically."[7]

Walter Laqueur offers a very broad definition of terrorism as "the use of covert violence by a group for political ends."[8] Caleb Carr also defines terrorism broadly, in this case as war with one distinction: it is "warfare deliberately waged against civilians with the purpose of destroying their will to support either leaders or policies that the agents of such violence find objectionable." Carr makes no distinction between conventional military and unconventional paramilitary forces because, for him,

> Anyone who asserts that a particular armed force or unit or individual that deliberately targets civilians in the pursuit of a political goal is for some reason not an exponent of terrorism…is rather concerned with excusing the behavior of the nation or faction for whom he or she feels sympathy.[9]

Others have argued for more restrictive definitions. By acknowledging the long history of terrorism as an activity of states, Bruce Hoffmann, for example, defines modern terrorism as politically motivated violence or threatened violence "perpetrated by a subnational group or nonstate entity" with an "identifiable chain of command or conspiratorial cell structure (whose members wear no uniform or identifying insignia)."[10] This definition restricts terrorism to substate or nonstate entities with specific command or cell structures. Others, for example, Schmid and Jongman, have offered even more complicated definitions.[11]

The conceptual problem is exacerbated by what Hoffman calls the "pejorative" nature of the term[12] and by a tendency on the part of many to rationalize what Marshall has described as "a distinction between civil and uncivil violence: (useless) terror and (useful) enforcement, (undisciplined) terrorism and (disciplined) war, (dishonorable) terrorists and (honorable) freedom fighters.[13] Cunningham points out that by nature terrorism is an "emotionally laden phenomenon."[14] Although scholars may use the term as a "research category," policy makers tend to use it as an "evaluative" one.[15] In the latter case, what might appear to be terrorism to one group might not be considered terrorism by a different group. As Hoffman observes,

> If one identifies with the victim of violence, for example, then the act is terrorism. If, however, one identifies with the perpetrator, the violent act is regarded as more sympathetic, if not in a positive (or at worst, ambivalent) light; and it is not terrorism.[16]

In general, government labeling of terrorism tends to be influenced by policy considerations. This can result in what Dennis Sandole calls a "privileging" of one side (governments) at the expense of another (those labeled as terrorists).[17] Moreover, governments are typically reluctant to label as terrorist a group whose cause they regard as just or to whom they are providing material assistance.[18]

These considerations have led terrorism experts such as Brian Jenkins to declare that terrorism must be defined by "the quality of the act and not by the identity of the perpetrator or the nature of their cause."[19]

From a definitional perspective, scholars have focused on different aspects of the phenomenon. Walter Laqueur's definition, though broad, focuses on four key characteristics of terrorism:

1. It is violent.
2. It is covert, not conventional war.
3. It is collective, not just individual.
4. It is political, not simply criminal.

Martha Crenshaw also stresses the political nature of terrorism. However, she focuses on the psychological, symbolic, and communicative features of the act. She describes the phenomenon as

> The systematic use of unorthodox violence by small conspiratorial groups with the purpose of manipulating political attitudes rather than physically defeating an enemy. The intent of terrorist violence is psychological and symbolic, not material. Terrorism is premeditated and purposeful violence, employed in a struggle for political power. As Harold Lasswell defined it: "Terrorists are participants in the political process who strive for political results by arousing acute anxieties."[20]

Others have zeroed in on the anxiety- or fear-producing quality of terror to demarcate it from other types of violence. Brian Jenkins, for example, defines terrorism as "violence or the threat of violence calculated to create an atmosphere of fear and alarm—in a word to terrorize—and thereby bring about some social or political change."[21] Enders and Sandler in their work also emphasize the importance of the creation of fear and intimidation as a key attribute of terrorism. They define terrorism as

> Premeditated use or threat of use of extranormal violence or brutality by subnational groups to gain a political, religious or ideological objective through intimidation of a huge audience, usually not directly involved with the policy making that the terrorists seek to influence.[22]

According to these definitions, the immediate targets of violence may be government personnel or resources, but often the victims are private citizens and property. Terrorists may bomb schools or restaurants, kill tourists, or take contractors hostage to spread fear in a public and influence governments and other organizations to give in to their demands. They may act independently or be state sponsored. Their goals, moreover, may be nationalist, separatist, leftist, rightist, anarchic, or even religious.[23]

These definitions include acts of terrorism, whether states or nonstate groups or entities conduct the acts. U.S. government definitions, on the other hand, take a more variable approach. The Department of Defense defines terrorism as

> The unlawful use of—or threatened use of—force or violence against individuals or property to coerce or intimidate governments or societies, often to achieve political, religious, or ideological objectives.[24]

This definition does not exclude terrorism conducted by states. On the other hand, the Department of State and the Central Intelligence Agency both employ a definition that restricts terrorism to acts perpetrated by substate actors or clandestine agents. They define terrorism as

> Premeditated, politically motivated violence perpetrated against noncombatant targets by subnational groups or clandestine agents, usually intended to influence an audience.[25]

These definitional and perceptual problems are further exacerbated by a multiplicity of typologies of terrorism. Popular typologies tend to focus on terrorism perpetrated by nonstate actors. Such typologies may divide terrorist acts by motivation (including political and ideological), tactics, targets, or other schema.[26] Terrorism has also been classified in terms of broad dichotomies such as macro or superterrorism and microterrorism.[27] Although such classifications may be useful for specific purposes, they are often too complex to be useful in research.

Almost all definitions exclude crimes purely motivated by private gain such as blackmail, murder, or physical assault without any political objectives. However, determining whether an act of violence is or is not political is not always as easy as it seems.

Without minimizing the actuality of state-perpetrated terrorism, in this book I restrict the use of the term to the calculated or strategic use of violence or threatened violence by substate or nonstate actors to influence an audience for political gains. This definition has the advantage of addressing important relevant attributes of terrorism and excluding ones that are irrelevant. It is also close to the definition used by the U.S. State Department. In addition, it is similar to the one used by Enders and Sandler in previous quantitative studies. Finally, because it focuses on the strategic and political nature of terrorism, it places the phenomenon within the realm of other nonstate strategies of violence (e.g., protest, guerilla war) used by insurgent actors for political ends. This is especially important for this book since, at least until recently, attention to strategy in the terrorism literature has been rare and insights from other literatures, for example, social movement/resource mobilization and asymmetric war theory, may shed light on the problem at hand.

WHAT IS TRANSNATIONAL TERRORISM?

Domestic terrorism is usually defined as homegrown terrorism. Its perpetrators and its targets/victims, according to this definition, both come from the same home country. International or transnational terrorism, on the other hand, is thought to involve perpetrators and victims from more than one country. For many years, the term *international* terrorism was used to distinguish between purely domestic incidents and those not limited to the internal affairs of individual states. Wilkinson, for example, defined terrorism as international when it is (1) directed at foreigners or foreign targets, (2) conducted by the governments or factions of more than one state, or (3) aimed at influencing the policies of a foreign government.[28]

The U.S. Central Intelligence Agency labeles terrorism as *international* when its "ramifications transcend national boundaries (as the result, for example, of the nationality or foreign ties of its perpetrators, its locale, the identity of its institutional or human victims, its declared objectives or the mechanics of its resolution)."[29] More recently, the term *transnational* terrorism has come into use to refer to terrorist acts that begin in one country and end in another or are perpetrated by citizens of one country against foreign targets within that country or abroad. As Enders and Sandler clarify,

> When an incident is planned in one country but executed in another, it is a transnational event. The kidnapping or assassination of a citizen from another country in a host country is also a transnational terrorist act, as is a bombing directed at one or more foreign citizens.

In addition, the hijacking of a plane that takes off in one country but is planned to land in another is transnational. In addition, if the flight has passengers on it from more than one country, even if it is on the ground, an attack on that plane could be considered transnational.[30]

Today, the U.S. State Department in its annual publication *Patterns of Global Terrorism* uses both terms, *international* and *transnational*, apparently interchangeably. However, determining when an event is truly transnational as opposed to domestic is not always as simple as it might appear. One of the characteristics of terrorism is secrecy. As a result, if a foreign perpetrator does not claim an act, or a foreign perpetrator is not identified, one might not actually know if the act is transnational or domestic. Moreover, there may be considerable debate over whether the "ramifications" of an act place it in the domestic or international/transnational category.

In this book, I use the term *domestic terrorism* to refer to terrorist acts and threats in which the perpetrators and victims are from one country. I use the term *transnational terrorism*, in the way described by Enders and Sandler, to refer to terrorist acts and threats in which the perpetrators and targets or victims are from different countries.

WHAT IS "ISLAMIST" TERRORISM?

One of the goals of this book is to look at the impact of the War on Terrorism on transnational terrorist activity perpetrated by Islamist organizations or for Islamist causes. It is, therefore, necessary to discuss some of the difficulties implicit in the use of these terms.

The term *Islamist* is generally used to refer to individuals and groups who promote Islamic religious, social, and political causes through activism. Islamist causes may be personal and religious; for example, the promotion of a personal Islamic religious experience or adherence to particular Islamic religious traditions. Islamist causes, however, may also be social; for example, the promotion of Islamic social and cultural clubs and societies in universities. Or, they may be political; for example, the promotion of varying degrees of Islamic politics, including not only the adoption or extension of Sharia law but also the potential overthrow of a secular government and its replacement by an Islamist state.[31] In addition, Islamist causes may be foreign policy related; for example, the liberation of Palestine, the removal of foreign troops from occupied Islamic lands, or they may refer simply to the removal of foreign (non-Islamic) influences from a state or region. It should be noted that whereas Islamist causes are often related to the Islamic religion, it is not the case that they necessarily support strictly religious political solutions. Although supporters of Hezbollah in Lebanon often describe themselves as Islamists, they do not generally advocate the establishment of a theocratic state but rather a Western modeled secular one.[32]

Activism may take a number of forms including individual persuasion, participation in organized meetings, social and political forums to promote Islamic solutions to social, economic, or political problems, marches and protests, or, at the extreme end, involvement in radical extremist "Jihadi" Islamist groups that employ violence, including terrorism, to promote Islamist causes and solutions.

It needs to be emphasized that although lists of such groups have been compiled by sources such as the State Department and RAND, they are not comprehensive. Also, it is important to point out that some Islamist radical groups, although known as terrorist groups because they are associated with terrorism, also promote Islamic causes in nonviolent ways (through charities and other suborganizations). A typical example would be Hamas. Finally, because terrorism by nature is secretive and it is in the interest of terrorists to escape detention, they do not always claim the acts they perpetrate. As a result, terrorism perpetrated for Islamist causes in particular is not always readily attributable to an identifiable Islamist radical group.

What Is the War on Terrorism?

Defining the nature and meaning of the War on Terrorism also poses difficulties because of the multiple ways in which the U.S. administration has characterized it. From the time of Carl von Clausewitz, it has been an axiom that

> The first, the supreme, most far-reaching act of judgment that the statesman and the commander have to make is to establish the kind of war on which they are embarking, neither mistaking it for, nor trying to turn it into, something that is alien to its true nature.[33]

However, the nature of the War on Terrorism has never been specified in a way that is entirely clear. In the immediate aftermath of the September 11 attacks on the World Trade Center and the Pentagon, the president declared a "war against terrorism of global reach." Soon afterwards, he and others in his administration used the terms *global war on terrorism, war on global terrorism, war on terrorism, war on terror*, and *battle against international terrorism*. Although the term *global war on terrorism*, with its acronym, GWOT, became the one most frequently used, its meaning remains elusive. Is the emphasis on "global war" or on "global terrorism?" And is the target terrorism or terrorists or something else? From the outset, the administration specified what Jeffrey Record of the Strategic Studies Institute has called "a multiplicity of enemies, including rogue states, weapons of mass destruction (WMD) proliferators, terrorist organizations, and terrorism itself." Moreover, the administration more often than not merged terrorism and rogue states such as Iraq into "a single, undifferentiated terrorist threat."[34] In addition, although the administration frequently characterized this war as a military operation, it expanded the definition of war, in this case, to include intelligence, diplomacy, and police work.

Early on, the president clarified that this would be "a new kind of war."[35] As U.S. Secretary of Defense Rumsfeld put it as early as September 27, 2001, "this will be a war like none other our nation has faced.... Our opponent is a global network of terrorist organizations and their state sponsors.... Even the vocabulary of this war will be different."[36]

These considerations make defining this war very difficult. As Record points out, traditional wars involve military operations between states for control of the state or territory. In these cases, the means of war is combat between military forces and the end is military destruction of one side or the other. The GWOT was initially declared as a war against terrorism. Terrorists, however, do not field regular military forces or pursue territorial ends and "given their secretive, cellular, dispersed, and decentralized 'order of battle,' they are not subject to conventional military destruction." As a result, police and intelligence work often play a primary role in combating such organizations whereas military operations take a secondary position. Moreover, traditional wars have beginnings and endings; for example, when one or another side agrees to a ceasefire or peace agreement. Also, in traditional wars, there are conventional means of measuring success; for example, the amount of territory gained or tallies of enemies killed or captured. Such measures have little utility, as Record observes, in wars against shadowy, dispersed irregular forces such as al Qaeda and its associated organizations.[37]

Such observations may be responsible for the subtle shift, noted by the press and condoned by experts such as Kim Holmes of the Heritage Foundation in July 2005, when several members of the administration began to use the term *struggle* as opposed to *war* to refer to the current campaign against terrorism.[38] The president, however, rapidly made it clear that *war* not *struggle* was his preferred term.[39]

For this reason, and because the War on Terrorism has been conducted with an emphasis on its military operations, I characterize it as a war, even if an unconventional one. However, for the purpose of the study presented here, I focus on its impact on terrorist incidents rather than on terrorist organizations or other targets such as rogue states or states that harbor terrorists. In addition, I define the Global War on Terrorism in chronological terms beginning with the president's declaration of war in the aftermath of September 11, 2001, and extending through the invasion of Afghanistan (Operation Enduring Freedom), as well as the subsequent military operation in Iraq (Operation Iraqi Freedom). Although the latter operation was officially declared a victory when the regime of Saddam Hussein was removed in May 2003, operations against insurgents are still ongoing in that arena and these operations are generally considered a part of the GWOT. For logistical reasons, I limit the time frame to the period up through December of 2004.

CHAPTER 4

THE ORIGINS OF TERRORISM AND COUNTERTERRORISM

EXPLAINING TERRORISM

> Whenever a theory appears to you as the only possible one,
> take this as a sign that you have neither understood the theory
> nor the problem which it was intended to solve.[1]
>
> —Karl Popper

There has been a long tradition of explaining terrorism, including terrorism perpetrated by Islamist groups, in terms of grievance and psychosocial models. More recently, there has been a trend, especially in econometric studies, to focus on explanations based on rational choice, opportunity, and resource models. In addition, there has been a trend, especially in social movement and political action theory, to zero in on terrorist violence as a "tactic of contention" and a means of "resource mobilization" in wider conflicts.

These more recent models are especially relevant to the current study because, in addition to focusing on resources, they focus on strategy and tactics and the importance of evaluating outcomes in contentious conflicts. Nonetheless, all three models help shed light on the problem.

Early Models: Structural Strain and Grievance

Early studies of terrorism often focused on why individuals turned to violence. Several models, based on functionalism, focused on the problem of structural strain and concomitant grievance. An underlying assumption in these models is that societies are systems that have a tendency toward equilibrium and, in the normal course of events, societal demands are met by responsive institutions that, in turn, maintain equilibrium. According to functionalist models, disequilibrium occurs as a result of external strain, especially structural strain, which produces frustration, which, in turn, erupts in violence.[2]

Structural strain was conceptualized in a variety of ways but most often in terms of economic strain, political repression, and modernization. Only one scholar, as far as I can tell, tried to explain why terrorism as opposed to other kinds of violence (e.g., mob violence, rioting, lynching) occurred under conditions of strain. This was Senechal de la Roche, who argued that terrorism was more likely when structural strain was prolonged or widespread (and, hence, frustration and grievance were intense) but those considered responsible for the strain were socially distant from those most affected. This social distance, argued Senechal de la Roche, made it possible for the perpetrators of terrorism to conduct operations in a way that was cold, deliberate, and calculating, and it also made it possible for them to dehumanize their victims. In contrast, she argued that mob violence was more likely to occur when the strain was relatively recent while lynching, which is more personal, occurred when those who felt most aggrieved were in closer social proximity to their victims.[3]

Other scholars, using sociopsychological models, tried to explain terrorism in relation to the sense of isolation and impotence brought about by broad social changes. They posited that it is just this sense of isolation and impotence that leads individuals to join extremist groups, including terrorist ones. This approach is common in studies of what has come to be called "Islamist" terrorism. In such analyses, this genre of terrorism is often attributed to crises produced by the strains brought about by modernization and secularism. Rapid modernization is blamed, in particular, for concentrating wealth among a few and polarizing populations in the Islamic world. This polarization between the haves (mostly Western educated and secular) and the have-nots has led, it is argued, to a growing sense of impotence, made all the stronger by the Arab defeat in the 1967 War with Israel, among the masses.[4] Wiktorowicz points out that scholars have differed over the relative importance of social and economic variables versus imperialism as the producers of discomfort and, thus, of violence. In addition, he observes that they often part ways over the extent to which political repression and authoritarian rule at home are important to the model.[5] However, almost all posit direct relationships between variables such as structural strain, discomfort, and grievance, on the one hand, and violence in the form of terrorism on the other. Some scholars have even gone so far as to contend that the degree of Islamist violence is a function of the intensity of the crisis in the Islamic world.[6]

Strain-based explanations for terrorism, including Islamist terrorism, however, have been faulted for being fragile empirically. Structural strain exists almost everywhere in the world but only in some places at some times does it lead specifically to terrorism rather than other violent outcomes or no violent outcomes. Moreover, terrorism is not simply a release valve in the way that rioting might be for strain. As Crenshaw pointed out as early as 1981, terrorism is politically purposive.[7] It is also organized. And despite some arguments to the contrary,[8] its perpetrators are not simply isolated "dysfunctional" individuals seeking comfort. In fact, most of the research has shown that members of terrorist groups have higher levels of education than their peers and at least appear relatively well adjusted.

Rational Choice and Realist Models

In recent years, grievance and strain-based explanations have given way, especially in the econometric literature, to rational choice and opportunity models of terrorism. In these models, to which realists also increasingly subscribe,[9] terrorists are viewed as rational actors who, in Enders and Sandler's terms, "attempt to maximize a shared goal subject to a resource constraint."[10] According to this view, those who engage in terrorism are not simply dysfunctional but calculating and deliberate. As Sandler and Enders have put it, they want to "maximize utility or expected utility derived from the consumption of basic commodities produced from terrorist and non terrorist activities."[11] The utility may be media publicity, an atmosphere of intimidation, a concession or political instability, which comes about as a result of a terrorist act (e.g., bombing or skyjacking).[12]

In this model, terrorists deliberately choose strategies to maximize the effects (utility) they want but are subject to resource availability or "constraint." The choices may include how lethal an act to conduct, where to conduct it, the method to use, and who or what to target.[13] The resources they draw on may be natural ones or socially derived. The ready availability of diamonds (as existed in Sierra Leone) has been linked to terrorism. So have illegal social institutions (e.g., transnational criminal networks). In addition, legal institutions (legitimate businesses, religious and social organizations, and even charities) may be important resources for terrorism.[14] Terrorists, however, are subject to constraints. They may be constrained by the amount of capital they can raise. They may be further constrained by the presence of different levels of commitment or divergent agendas of middlemen they employ to raise money or carry out operations.[15] The main point here is that terrorists are rational and resource limited. They *choose* tactics and targets based on their own goals and how they may calculate they can achieve one goal or another, but their ability to carry out specific actions may be limited by the resources they have available.

Social Movement and Resource Mobilization Models

Like rational choice models, social movement and resource mobilization models emphasize the rational and purposive aspects of tactics in contentious collective encounters. Although these models were originally developed to explain nonviolent protest movements (e.g., civil rights and women's rights movements) in largely democratic societies, they are beginning to turn their expertise toward other kinds of movements, including violent ones.[16]

Early on, scholars in this field, such as McAdam, took exception to functionalist models of collective action based solely on strain and grievance. They pointed out that systems are not static or balanced but often changing and dynamic. They also observed that although structural strain and discontent exist almost everywhere, only sometimes do such conditions lead to collective action or movements. In addition, they observed that movements, such as the civil rights movement, were focused and purposeful and that individuals who joined such movements were not simply dysfunctional but often educated well-adjusted members of society.[17]

Focusing on the purposive and organized nature of contentious movements, scholars in the field began to turn their attention to the strategic aspects of contention and the importance of resources for mobilization.[18] Early on, scholars of the civil rights movement, such as McAdam, had emphasized the importance of the church as a mobilizing institution for black insurgency.[19] More recently, institutions such as the mosque, as well as professional and student associations, have been identified as mobilizing structures and resources for Islamist movements.[20] Although Islamists have traditionally rejected political participation as not being Islamic, there is evidence of increasing use of political organizations in such movements, and the role of political parties as a resource for mobilization is also being identified in the literature.[21]

Perhaps most important for this book is the increasing focus among a few scholars in this field on Islamist violence as a "tactic of contention" in Islamist movements. Work by Quintan Wiktorowicz (2001) on Islamist contention in Jordan, Glen Robinson (2003) on Hamas, Munson (2001) on the Muslim Brotherhood and Mohammed Hafez (2004) on Islamist violence in Algeria and Egypt are especially relevant because this body of work shows that violence related to Islamist movements does not occur in a vacuum but occurs under specific conditions and that tactical choices by groups as varied as Hamas, the Muslim Brotherhood, the GIA, and the Gama'a Islamiyya are uniquely responsive to conditions, including the tactics of governments.[22]

Strategic Calculations

Terrorists have been described as "rational actors who employ violence or threats of violence to promote their political goals and who derive utility and incur costs from undertaking terrorist acts."[23] According to this view, terrorism is undertaken for a variety of reasons. Terrorists may simply want to gain a concession such as the release of prisoners. They may seek media attention to make a cause more widely known.[24] They may intend to destabilize a polity or damage an economy to impose costs on a population and thereby force them to comply with their demands.[25] In many cases, there may be multiple agendas and multiple goals.[26] Terrorists seek to achieve such goals using a variety of means. They may stage targeted attacks; for example, assassinations of political leaders. They may attack targets of symbolic value (e.g., embassies), or they may attempt to spread fear and panic in a population by attacking civilians at random. In addition, they may use a variety of methods including hostage taking, bombing, suicide attacks, murder, assassination, arson, and threats. Such acts may be domestic or transnational.

Like other contending groups, terrorists face resource constraints. They may be constrained at the outset in terms of weapons, training, funds, or manpower. In addition, their resources may be depleted in the course of a terrorist campaign or as a result of counterterrorist efforts. These considerations have led some analysts to observe that to achieve the same purposes, terrorists, faced with resource constraints, may substitute one form of attack for another. For example, Enders and Sandler found that in response to the installation of metal detectors, skyjackings decreased but kidnappings increased. They attributed this phenomenon to a "substitution effect."[27] On the other hand, faced with resource constraints, those who engage in terrorism may find novel means of attack to draw publicity and create additional support. They may even engage in more brutal methods (such as the beheadings witnessed in 2004 in Iraq) to provoke an overreaction that may help win new supporters.[28]

EXPLAINING COUNTERTERRORISM

The concept of counterterrorism is generally defined within specific frames of terrorism. In one frame, terrorism may be defined as crime. In this case, counterterrorism tends to be defined prescriptively in terms of police and law enforcement work. On the other hand, when terrorism is defined in terms of war or revolution, counterterrorism tends to be prescribed in terms of military responses. Prescriptively, defensive and offensive (proactive) responses have both been recommended as measures to defeat terrorism.[29]

In general, counterterrorist campaigns are mounted with the specific goal of raising the costs to terrorists of mounting attacks. Governments may try to make terrorist attacks more difficult through defensive measures (e.g., tightening security or tightening penalties) or through offensive ones (e.g., police and military raids or assassinations or other covert operations) to take out operatives, destroy weapons and training facilities, and reduce the funds terrorists rely on.

Defensive responses have included erecting technological barriers, fortifying targets (e.g., embassies, bridges), and increasing surveillance. Laws (e.g., the Antiterrorism Laws of 1984 and more recently the Patriot Act), which increase penalties for consorting with or contributing to terrorism, are other examples of defensive responses. In addition, international agreements have been employed as means of defending against terrorism through sharing of intelligence and squeezing of potential methods terrorists may use to raise and transfer funds.

Offensive responses have included military actions (retaliatory and preemptive strikes) and covert actions, including infiltration and even assassinations. Significant offensive actions taken by the United States include its strikes against Libya in 1986, its strikes against al Qaeda training camps in Afghanistan and Pakistan, its preemptive strikes against Iraq in 1998, and, more recently, the coalition action known as Operation Enduring Freedom targeting al Qaeda training camps in Afghanistan, as well as Operation Iraqi Freedom. The policy of preemption articulated by the U.S. government in the immediate aftermath of the September 11, 2001, attacks is also in line with the latter approach. Governments, however, face a trade-off, as Bueno de Mesquita points out. They must always "balance the security benefits of counterterrorism against the costs in terms of mobilizing potential terrorists."[30] It may be for this reason that the U.S. government has used force only rarely in response to international terrorist incidents.[31]

DOES FORCE ESCALATE TERRORISM?

Contending Theories

A fundamental tenet of collective action theory is that in the face of organized violence "soft" responses have the effect of increasing such activity whereas "harder" more forceful ones make it more difficult for challengers to conduct their operations.[32]

Whether the use of hard tactics actually decreases oppositional violence, however, is a matter of debate.[33] Offensive measures may be undertaken to prevent future terrorist attacks. Such tactics, however, may have competing effects. On the one hand, they may make it more difficult for terrorist organizations to recruit and operate. However, they can also have an escalating effect, for example, when they drive a hard core further underground where they become more focused and more deadly.[34] In addition, cracking down on contention may increase grievances and consequently terrorist recruitment.[35] Defensive moves on the part of government may also have competing effects. As Rosendorff and Sandler observe, such moves may increase the costs to terrorists of doing business but they may also impose external costs—as when "terrorists shift a planned attack to a nation taking the least precautions."[36]

The Empirical Evidence

> Weak people never give way when they ought to.
> —Cardinal de Retz

Quantitative Studies

Previous research using quantitative methods has shown that the use of massive force as a counterterrorism strategy has not had the desired effect of reducing terrorism and in some cases has been counterproductive. One study assessed the effect of Israeli raids following a series of Palestinian attacks against Israelis. The raids included the Israeli attack on PLO bases in Syria after the Black September massacre of athletes during the 1972 Olympic Games, the attack on Palestinian guerrilla bases in Lebanon after the March 1978 Haifa bus hijacking, and the bombing of Palestinian guerrilla bases in Lebanon after the June 1982 assassination attempt against the Israeli ambassador in London. These raids were shown to have a short-term effect on the frequency of terrorist attacks perpetrated by Palestinians in the months afterwards. However, within 9 months it showed that the average number of attacks had returned to the same level as before the raids.[37] Another study examined the effects of the U.S. raid on Libya in 1986. The results of this study indicated that the raid had the unintended consequence of actually raising the level of terrorism at least in the near term.[38] More recently, the use of extended force, including border closings and bombings, by the Israeli government has been shown to have inflamed Palestinian public opinion and only further mobilized support for militants.[39] On the other hand, flexible policies combining a measure of responsiveness with an emphasis on law and public order have been shown to reduce terrorist violence by Basque insurgents in Spain.[40]

Qualitative Work

The qualitative literature also lends support to the claim that the use of massive force against insurgent violence has escalating effects. In relation to Northern Ireland, Scott Woods observes that, in 1969, the British government sent in military troops to quell riots that had erupted there over civil rights. At this time, the Provisional Irish Republican Army (PIRA), which had mounted terrorist attacks in the past, was relatively inactive. Within a year, however, a "resurrected" and presumably more motivated PIRA was carrying out new attacks against the British troops.[41] Similar effects were observed in relation to the use of massive force to quell Islamic extremist acts of violence in Upper Egypt in the mid-1990s. In this case, Mohammad Hafez and Quintan Wiktorowicz found that the government of Egypt overreacted, casting too wide a net, a tactic which had the effect of increasing a sense of victimization and sympathy for the organizational causes and tactics of terrorism and legitimatizing such tactics.[42] Evidence from a case comparison study of militant Islamist opposition in Central Asia lends further support to the theory that heavier tactics as opposed to lighter ones are associated with more terrorism rather than less. In this instance, McGlinchey attributes the much higher number of suicide attacks by Islamists in Uzbekistan compared with Kyrgyzstan to its increasingly tight military control and more frequent and indiscriminate use of force to quell opposition.[43] On the other hand, the more "managerial" tactics used by the government of Jordan were found, in a case study by Quintan Wiktorowicz, to moderate Islamist opposition, although such tactics were also found to divert opponents into informal networks.[44] The results of studies such as these and others have led scholars such as Goldstone and Tilly to conclude that the employment of force as a counterinsurgent and counterterrorist strategy almost always leads to increased challenges and not the reverse.[45]

Refinements in Theory

Insights from a variety of literatures suggest that the impact of force as a counterinsurgent or counterterrorist method may be modified by other variables. Some scholars have suggested that the level of force is key.[46] As noted in the following, others have focused on the level of discrimination of force. Still others have argued that whether force is accompanied by other shifts (e.g., an expansion of issues and parties) or whether it disintegrates into "barbarism" may be what is critical to escalation.

Insights From the Social Movement Literature

In their analyses of counterterrorist and counterinsurgent efforts in Algeria and Egypt, Hafez and Wiktorowicz found that high levels of force, applied indiscriminately (as when noninsurgents, as well as insurgents, were targeted), were more likely than more selective levels of force to have an escalatory effect. They observe that the selective use of force signals to supporters and sympathizers that only "troublemakers" will be targeted. On the other hand, indiscriminate force, casting a wide net, has the potential to inflame and mobilize sympathizers and supporters. In such situations, "moral outrages" committed by militants may be perceived as the "natural response to indiscriminate repression."[47] In support of this hypothesis, these authors cite the findings of Gurr and Goldstone, who observed that American bombings of Cambodian and Vietnamese villages suspected of aiding rebels had an inflammatory effect and drove peasants to join the ranks of revolutionary armies.[48] In addition, they cite Horne, who demonstrated that French policies of "collective responsibility" during Algeria's war of independence (1954–1962) led to an increase in membership in organizations such as the National Liberation Front (FLN).[49]

Contributions From the Conflict Literature

Insights from the conflict literature lend support to the claim that the use of hard or heavy tactics has an escalatory effect on domestic contention and conflict. Building on the classic work of conflict scholar, Morton Deutsch,[50] Dean Pruitt, and Jeffrey Rubin observe that escalation tends to be greatest when other factors also operate. They point to the importance of five factors. First, there is a shift from "light to heavy tactics." Second, the conflict grows in size. Third, the number of issues expands and parties begin to see the other side as "evil." Fourth, the number of parties proliferates as more and more people are drawn into the conflict. And fifth, goals on either or both sides change from "doing well" to winning and finally hurting the other.[51] Moreover, grievances, feelings of injustice, and high levels of frustration add to escalation and lead to a "conflict spiral" producing a sense of crisis,[52] and it is argued, "once these transformations have taken place, escalation tends to persist and recur." In such situations, even other latent conflicts may become manifest, fueling what Dennis Sandole has called an aggressive manifest conflict process.[53]

In some cases, according to Karklins and Peterson, severe repression may become a "focal event" that marks a critical tipping point[54] and has a cascading effect.[55] Francisco points out that backlash is a common occurrence after episodes of severe repression, for example, the massacre of 530 people at Amritsar, India, in 1919, the Soweto massacre in which as many as 1,000 were killed in South Africa in 1976, and the killing of 13 people on Bloody Sunday in Derry, Northern Ireland, in 1972. In these cases, the aftermath was one of greater mobilization, a struggle against the state, and guerilla war.[56]

Evidence From the Asymmetric War Literature

Additional support for the contention that massive force is likely to be counterproductive when used against substate or nonstate insurgents is provided in the asymmetric war literature. Again, however, there are refinements to theory. According to Arreguin-Toft, force per se may not be as critical as "strategic interaction." Departing from Mack's contention that will or resolve is the most important issue in asymmetric conflicts,[57] Arreguin-Toft hypothesizes that what is critical is "strategic interaction." By strategy, he means "an actor's plan for using armed forces to achieve military or political objectives." By "strategic interaction," he means the interaction between the strategies of actors.[58]

Arreguin-Toft argues that actors in asymmetric conflicts tend to use either "direct attack" or "indirect attack."[59] In many cases, strong actors (governments) are attracted to direct approaches (attrition or blitzkrieg) designed to destroy a weaker actor's capacity to fight. On the other hand, weak actors often employ indirect approaches (guerilla war and terrorism) to wear down and erode their opponents' will.[60] Such strategies, which focus on stealth, mobility, surprise, and deception, were central in Mao's strategy against the Japanese army and the Nationalist government of China:

> When you want to fight us, we don't let you and you can't find us. But when we want to fight you, we make sure that you can't get away and we hit you squarely... and wipe you out. The enemy advances, we retreat; the enemy camps, we harass; the enemy tires, we attack; the enemy retreats, we pursue.[61]

In his analysis of more than 200 asymmetric conflicts, he found that strong actors employing "direct" methods of military force (attrition or blitzkrieg) almost always fared poorly against weak actors when the latter employed "indirect" methods (e.g., guerilla war or terrorism). He attributes these results to the fact that weak actors, when using indirect methods, have the advantage of time whereas stronger actors risk looking incompetent. In addition, he suggests that strong actors may become impatient and resort to "barbarism," which he defines as the violation of traditional laws of war, for example, indiscriminate bombings, rape, murder, or torture.[62] These insights may be particularly relevant to this study since terrorism, like guerrilla warfare, has been defined as a form of irregular warfare or "small war."[63] Also, the evidence of photos of U.S. soldiers abusing prisoners at the Abu Ghraib prison in April 2004 suggests that in some instances at least the U.S. effort did disintegrate into barbaric behavior.

THE PROBLEM OF TRANSNATIONAL TERRORISM

Although the relationship between force and domestic insurgence and terrorism has been a subject of growing research attention, comparatively less attention has been paid to the impact of force on transnational terrorism.

Dilemmas for Governments and Terrorists

Transnational terrorism poses a number of collective action problems for governments. Targeted countries may work together or not work together to combat a terrorist threat. Some countries may decide to free ride to avoid being a target. Terrorist organizations also have collective action problems, which they may solve by working together and sharing resources. Such cooperative action may present further problems for governments facing a more coordinated threat. In addition to choosing whether or not to work in concert, targeted governments have to choose between different strategies to combat terrorism. In general, governments want to increase the cost of terrorism so as to make it less likely. Governments, however, face trade-offs. They may chose largely defensive policies such as securing borders, airports, and major installations. Such policies, however, are expensive and it is virtually impossible for a government to secure every vulnerable point in its homeland or its interests abroad. Moreover, as Sandler points out, "terrorists bent on mass destruction only have to be successful once whereas society must be fortunate daily to avoid such a catastrophe."[64] Alternatively, governments may choose offensive strategies. However, in this case, they have to weigh the benefits against the costs in terms of potential mobilization of terrorists.

In response to government actions, terrorists also face choices. They may choose to adapt to defensive measures by ceasing their activities. Alternatively, they may shift into new modes of attack or switch to new targets.[65] Terrorists also have a variety of choices in response to offensive measures designed to take out their operatives or reduce their resources. They may choose to cease their activities or go underground for a period. Alternatively, they may shift into lower cost activities, as Enders and Sandler suggest they did after the onset of 9/11. On the other hand, they may use the potentially inflaming effect of the counterterrorist measures to gather new support and increase the frequency, lethality, or dispersion of their attacks. In addition, insofar as governments choose to work in concert, those engaging in transnational terrorism may redirect their attacks to new enemies. For example, they could focus their attacks on coalitions of governments or other organizations involved in or supporting the counterterrorism effort.

Need for Research

Most of the research on the relationship between government strategies and subsequent terrorism has focused on domestic terrorism. An unresolved question is whether the use of force escalates or deescalates terrorist activity when the specific target is transnational terrorist activity.

Although a few studies have used quantitative methods to examine the effects of defensive policies on transnational terrorist activity,[66] only one quantitative study, to the author's knowledge, has tried to analyze whether 9/11 and the War on Terrorism have shifted or changed the pattern of transnational terrorist activity.[67] That study, however, is limited to one database (ITERATE) and since it is based in rational choice theory it focuses on shifts or "substitution effects" in terrorist activity rather than escalation. In addition, the analysis only extends through the second quarter of 2003. As a result, it does not have the ability to capture the longer-term and potentially mobilizing effects of events such as the invasion of Iraq in March 2003, the capture of Saddam Hussein in December 2003, and the release of photos of abuse from Abu Ghraib in April 2004.

There is a need for more research on the relationship between the use of force and transnational terrorist activity. This need is particularly pressing as this is written, at the end of 2005, since some members of the Bush administration are beginning to redefine the criteria by which success in the GWOT is measured. For example, in recent days, in relation to the war in Iraq (which has been described as a central front in the war on terrorism), U.S. Secretary of Defense Donald Rumsfeld stated,

> To be responsible, it seems to me, *one needs to stop defining success in Iraq as the absence of terrorist attacks.* As Senator Joe Lieberman recently suggested, a better measure of success might be that a vast majority of Iraqis, tens of millions, are on the side of the democratic government while a comparatively small number are opposed to that government.[68]

I disagree. Establishing a democratic government in Iraq may be a laudable goal. But the success of the war on terrorism needs to be measured in terms of terrorism and its incidence and not on other accomplishments. To score this war otherwise, in my opinion, is to change the rules.

PART II

WHEN TERRORISM AND COUNTERTERRORISM CLASH

CHAPTER 5

HOW DO WE MEASURE SUCCESS?

QUESTIONS, HYPOTHESES, AND THEORIES

> I gather, young man, that you wish to be a Member of Parliament.
> The first lesson that you must learn is, when I call for statis-
> tics about the rate of infant mortality, what I want is proof that
> fewer babies died when I was Prime Minister than when any-
> one else was Prime Minister. That is a political statistic.
> —Winston Churchill

The overarching question in this study is whether the military
effort, known as the GWOT, has changed the frequency or nature
of transnational terrorist activity. In addressing this question and
subquestions about the effects of the invasion of Iraq, the capture
of Saddam Hussein, and the release of photos from Abu Ghraib,
I use a quantitative approach. However, unlike Winston Churchill
in the aforementioned anecdote, I hope to uncover real answers,
not just "political statistic(s)."

Hypotheses

Rational choice models of terrorism suggest that terrorists operate within resource constraints and rationally calculate the utility of actions based on the benefits of such activities and their own resources and constraints. On the basis of these models, one might expect those who engage in terrorism to respond to offensive measures, designed to take out their resources, by *decreasing* such activity, or by shifting into different less costly or less resource-intensive modes of attack.[1] Such models, however, ignore the potential inflaming or revolutionary effects of force as a counter-terrorism strategy.

Based on alternative resource mobilization models and evidence that in domestic situations force almost always has an inflaming and escalatory effect, I hypothesized that the military effort, known as the War on Terrorism, would show a similar effect on transnational terrorist activity. Specifically, I expected that it would be found to be associated with an increase in the frequency, lethality, and dispersion of such activity. These expectations can be stated as propositions.

> *Hypothesis 1:* The War on Terrorism has led to an increase in the average number of transnational terrorist incidents.
>
> *Hypothesis 2:* The War on Terrorism has led to an increase in the average number of days on which transnational terrorist incidents occur.
>
> *Hypothesis 3:* The War on Terrorism has led to an increase in lethal transnational terrorist incidents.
>
> *Hypothesis 4:* The War on Terrorism has led to an increase in the dispersion of transnational terrorist incidents.
>
> *Hypothesis 4a:* The War on Terrorism has led to an increase in the average number of countries where transnational terrorism occurs.

Hypothesis 4b: The War on Terrorism has led to an increase in the number of incidents in Muslim countries in general.

Hypothesis 4c: The War on Terrorism has led to an increase in incidents in the Middle East/North African region in particular.

In their study of transnational terrorist incidents after 9/11, Enders and Sandler argued that logistically complex types of attacks, such as hostage takings, should have decreased in absolute number and as a percentage of all types of attacks after the onset of the War on Terrorism and, indeed, their analysis of ITERATE data through 2003 found that this was the case.[2] It is possible, however, that this finding is not upheld when the analysis is extended through 2004 and more data are included. For this reason, I proposed:

Hypothesis 5: The War on Terrorism has led to an increase in the average number of hostage takings as an absolute number and as a percentage of all types of attacks.

Since the War on Terrorism has been a multinational effort with the participation and/or support of multiple nations, as well as multinational companies and organizations, I also hypothesized that it would be found to be associated with an expansion in the targets of transnational terrorist activity. Specifically, I expected that it would be found to have increased the targeting of multinational entities, including multinational companies, international government organizations such as the UN, and international NGOs such as the Red Cross and members of all such entities.

Hypothesis 6: The War on Terrorism has led to an increase in transnational terrorist incidents in which the victims are multinational (i.e., natives of more than one country) or organizations or members of such organizations as a percentage of all transnational terrorist incidents.

Since the War on Terrorism has been led by the United States and a main purpose of the effort has been to protect U.S. citizens, I further proposed:

> *Hypothesis 7:* The War on Terrorism has led to a decrease in transnational terrorist incidents in which one or more victims are U.S. citizens.

Since the War on Terrorism was focused on al Qaeda and its network of related and affiliated and associated "Islamist" organizations and such targeting could have had an inflaming effect, I also proposed:

> *Hypothesis 8:* The GWOT has led to an increase in transnational terrorist incidents perpetrated by known "Islamist" terrorist organizations.

Based on insights from conflict theory, which indicate that escalation occurs when the number of issues expands and the number of parties grows, I expected that the escalatory effects of the War on Terrorism would be greater for each of the provided variables after the invasion of Iraq in March 2003. Based on similar insights relating to "injustice frames," I expected that escalatory effects would be further magnified for each of the provided variables after the capture of Saddam Hussein in December 2003. In addition, on the basis of asymmetric war theory indicating that barbarism (i.e., violation of the laws of war) or the perception of barbarism is counterproductive in asymmetric conflicts, I hypothesized an additional escalatory effect following the release of photos of prisoner abuse of Iraqis by American troops at Abu Ghraib. These expectations can be stated as a further proposition.

Hypothesis 9: The following events associated with the War on Terrorism have led to an escalation in the frequency, lethality, dispersion, taking of hostages, and targeting of multinationals and U.S. citizens:

  (i) The invasion of Iraq in March 2003
  (ii) The capture of Saddam Hussein in December 2003
  (iii) The release of photos of abuse from Abu Ghraib prison in April 2004

RESEARCH METHODS

Design

To test these propositions, I use a quasiexperimental design, namely the time series intervention approach following the tradition advocated by Box and Tiao.[3] This approach is generally considered the strongest of the quasiexperimental approaches for evaluating the longitudinal effects of interventions. Daniel Druckman points out that the strength of this design "derives from the feature of multiple measures before and after an intervention."[4]

Although randomization is missing, the time series design enables a researcher to evaluate change in the context of a longer history of events. It also allows for an evaluation of the extent to which the change is sustained through time.[5]

Such designs have been described as appropriate for analyses of the impact of new economic policies on subsequent economic performance or for analyses of new anticrime legislation on subsequent crime rates.[6] They have been used to analyze the impact of environmental and policy issues.[7] They have also been used to analyze the marketing of new brand products[8] and even to assess the effects of a catastrophic event, Hurricane Hugo, on timber prices and ecosystems.[9] Most relevantly for the project at hand, time series intervention analyses have been employed to study the usefulness of military offensives versus mediation in response to violence in the former Soviet Union,[10] the effectiveness of retaliatory raids in response to terrorism,[11] the effects of UN conventions on terrorist activities,[12] the impact of news reporting on subsequent terrorist incidents,[13] and the impact of specific antiterrorist policies and defensive interventions on the incidence and choice of tactics of terrorism.[14]

In this design, the intervention variables are coded as dichotomous dummy variables (0, 1) to flag the occurrence (0 = *absence*, 1 = *presence*) of an event presumed to affect the response series. The event is viewed as an *intervention* or an *interruption* of the normal course of the response time series, which, in the absence of intervention, is assumed to be more or less stable. The interruption may be a one-time occurrence. For example, one could examine the effect of a weeklong government raid on domestic terrorism in the month following the raid. In this case, the input variable has the value of "1" for the time period during the raid and "0" for all other periods. Intervention variables of this kind are sometimes called *impulse* or *pulse* functions.

On the other hand, interventions may be continuing and the input variable may flag periods before and after the intervention. In this case, the input variable has the value of "1" after the intervention and the value of "0" before. Intervention variables such as these are called *step* functions.[15]

In this study, I examine the impact of the GWOT, coded as "0" starting with the October 7, 2001, invasion of Afghanistan, on subsequent terrorist activity. I also analyze the separate impact of other interventions including the invasion of Iraq in March 2003, the capture of Saddam Hussein in December 2003, and the release of shocking photos of prisoner abuse from Abu Ghraib in April 2004.

Independent Variables

The primary independent variable in this time series intervention analysis is

- The *War on Terrorism*, flagged as "1" from October 7, 2001 (the date of the start of military action in Afghanistan), to the ending date of the data analyzed (December 31, 2004) and as "0" for all other periods.[16]

The secondary independent variables include the following:

- The War in Iraq, flagged as "1" from March 20, 2003 (the date of the invasion of Iraq) to the ending date of the data analyzed (December 31, 2004) and as "0" for all other periods.
- The capture of Saddam Hussein, flagged as "1" from December 14, 2003 (the date of his capture) to the ending date of the data analyzed (December 31, 2004) and as "0" for all other periods. I make the assumption that the capture of Saddam Hussein had a persistent effect since it is known that former regime elements were still operative at the end of December 2004.
- The release of photos showing U.S. troops abusing Iraqi prisoners at Abu Ghraib, flagged as "1" from April 29, 2004 (the date of the first television airing of these photos) to the ending date of the data analyzed (December 31, 2004). Again, I make the assumption that the release of these photos had an ongoing mobilizing effect through 2004.

Dependent Variables

The focus of the analysis is on the impact of the War on Terrorism (and specific events associated with this campaign) on subsequent transnational terrorist activity, its frequency, lethality, dispersion, the type of attack, and the extent to which the victims are multinational.

I hypothesize that the GWOT (and specific events associated with the GWOT) has led to increases in the frequency and dispersion of terrorism, increased lethality per incident, and changes in type of attack (an increase in hostage taking) and changes in the type of victim (specifically an increase in multinational victims). To test these hypotheses, I extract quarterly time series data from existing terrorism event data sources.

For *frequency*, I extract two measures:

- Number of transnational terrorist incidents
- Number of days on which transnational terrorist incidents take place (This measure may be a good proxy for escalation as far as media attention since it is likely that terrorist incidents receive more attention when they are spread out on more days.)

For *dispersion*, I extract the following measures:

- Number of places (countries) in which transnational terrorist incidents take place
- Number of incidents in predominantly Muslim countries (countries with 50% or more Muslim populations) as a percentage of all incidents[17]
- Number of incidents in the Middle East and North Africa as a percentage of all incidents

For *lethality*, a number of variables could be used. One could examine the average number of casualties (deaths and/or injuries) in each quarterly period. Alternatively, one could examine the number of lethal incidents (those with deaths) or incidents with casualties (deaths or injuries). Since many incidents had deaths and injuries, I have decided to use the following measures:

- Number of lethal incidents (incidents with deaths)
- Number of incidents with casualties (deaths or injuries)

To capture incidents with multinational victims, I extract the number of incidents in which a multinational entity (multinational business, international organization such as the UN, international NGO such as the Red Cross), members of such an entity, or individuals from at least two different countries are the victims of an attack.

To assess change in type of attack, I extract three variables:

- Number of bombings
- Number of assassinations
- Number of hostage takings

To assess change in attacks by "Islamist" terrorist groups, I extract the following variable:

- Number of attacks claimed by or known to be perpetrated by radical Islamist and Islamist national separatist groups[18]

Units of Observation

One important issue in terms of units of observation is the choice of time intervals. Terrorism incident data have generally been collected on an event basis. Time series analysis, however, requires equally spaced units of observation (e.g., daily, monthly, quarterly, or annual intervals). Shorter intervals increase the potential number of observations but do so at a cost. Terrorism is not continuous. It often occurs in spurts, and when there is no terrorist event during a period, this is likely to lead to bias in time series estimates. Following previous work by Enders and Sandler,[19] I have chosen to use quarterly (3-monthly intervals) for the analysis because of the potential bias that could be introduced by missing values when no terrorism occurs. Since the RAND and ITERATE data sets from which the data are extracted both record incident data (sometimes several incidents per day, sometimes no incidents for a week or more), I have reformatted all of the data in quarterly intervals).

Choice of Time Span

Another important issue in terms of the units of observation is the choice of the time span from which the time series is extracted. Cook and Campbell have suggested that about 50 observations are ideal for such analyses, but an adequate analysis may use fewer observations depending on the expected impact of the intervention.[20] It has also been recommended that at least 20 of these observations occur prior to the intervention of interest. Larger numbers of observations are thought to be associated with smaller errors. However, lengthening the calendar time, before or after an intervention, can also lead to a situation in which other events (over and above those of interest) may be responsible for observed changes.

In a previous study, Enders and Sandler used ITERATE data from 1968 through mid-2003 to see if the frequency or lethality of all transnational terrorist incidents had changed after 9/11 as a "watershed event."[21] This analysis produced the finding that "little had changed." However, the authors did not specifically try to test whether there had been an increase in numbers of incidents. Rather, they focused on whether certain specified tactics as a proportion of tactics used in all incidents had changed in the period after 9/11. The authors did find that logistically complex hostage-taking incidents had fallen whereas logistically simple but deadly bombings had increased, but because the analysis did not extend into the second half of 2003 or include any data from 2004, it was unable to capture the potentially inflaming effects of the capture of Saddam Hussein and the release of photos from Abu Ghraib.

Moreover, by going back to 1968, the authors may have "watered down" attributes of terrorist incidents in the decade before 9/11, a decade that saw the end of the Cold War, the decline of many types of leftist and anarchist terrorism, and the rise of what some have called a "new kind of terrorism," which is more religiously motivated, less frequent, and more lethal.

Druckman observes that lack of positive findings in an interrupted time series design could indicate inadequate choice of a time period for analysis.[22] Since the War on Terrorism has specifically focused on al Qaeda and its associated groups and since I believe that the impact of the campaign should be measured in terms of changes in terrorist activity *since* the emergence of these particular groups, I chose to focus the empirical analyses of the effects of the War on Terrorism on a 12-year or 144-month time span from January 1, 1993, through December 31, 2004, a time frame that includes 8¾ years (35 quarters) before and 3¼ years (13 quarters) after the October 2001 invasion of Afghanistan, which is considered here as the start of the GWOT. As shown in Figure 1, this time frame allows for 48 observations or data points including 13 observations after and 35 observations before the onset of the War on Terrorism.

Figure 1. Time span and time intervals for study.

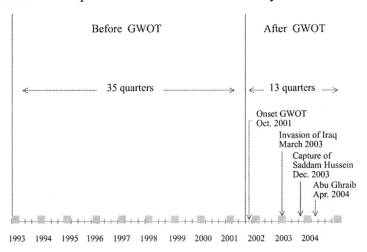

The ending date of the time frame (December 31, 2004) was chosen because it encompassed the most recent data available. The beginning date of the time frame (January 1, 1993) was chosen so that the analysis could focus as directly as possible on the years in which al Qaeda and its associated and related organizations, which are the target of the GWOT, have waged their global campaign.

Although al Qaeda (meaning "The Base") was formed in 1989, it appears to have used the years 1990 to 1992 to establish operational capacity, recruit members, and conduct training. During this period, numerous training camps were established in Afghanistan and elsewhere (Sudan, where Osama bin Laden settled in 1991, and Somalia). However, it was not until 1992 that al Qaeda's founder, Osama bin Laden, first called for jihad or "holy war."[23] In the ensuing months, it is now known that Mohammed Atef, an Egyptian aide to bin Laden, traveled to Somalia to organize violent attacks against U.S. and UN troops, which were carried out in 1993 when 18 American soldiers were attacked and killed in Mogadishu. The year 1993 saw the first World Trade Center bombing, an event that killed six and injured hundreds. This incident, which was linked to a blind Egyptian cleric who was the spiritual leader of Islamic Jihad, was later found to have received financial sponsorship from bin Laden and his al Qaeda group. It was also in 1993 that al Qaeda extended its activities to cells in Kenya, where it began to plot the embassy bombings that took place in 1998 and made plans to set up a media office in London, which it did in 1994.[24] In addition, the year 1993 saw the formation by alumni of al Qaeda of training camps of the Pakistani organization Harkat-ul-Ansar (later renamed Harka-al-Mujahideen), which has had numerous splinter groups and claims to have been active in Bosnia, Chechnya, India, Myanmar, the Philippines, and Tajikistan.[25] These considerations make the year 1993 a logical starting point for the analysis. However, to address any concern that an alternative starting point might produce different results, additional analyses with earlier and later starting points were also conducted.

SOURCES OF INFORMATION

> Errors using inadequate data are much less than those using no data at all.
>
> —Charles Babbage

Several sources of international/transnational terrorism incident data are available. They include the *International Terrorism: Attributes of Terrorist Events (ITERATE 1968–2003)*, a data set originally compiled by terrorism expert Edward Mickolus and updated by Todd Sandler, Jean M. Murdock, and Peter A. Fleming; the *RAND Terrorism Incident Database (RAND–MIPT 1968–2005)*, a textual database that updates the RAND–St. Andrews Chronology of International Terrorism, originating with terrorism experts Bruce Hoffman and Brian Jenkins, and is provided by the Oklahoma City Memorial Institute for the Prevention of Terrorism (MIPT) at http://www.mipt.org; the U.S. State Department Listing of Terrorist Incidents, available annually in the State Department publication *Patterns of Global Terrorism*; and the Pinkerton data set, which is available privately to some sources.

All these data sources are dependent on available news service sources and the human ability of compilers to capture terrorist incidents as they occur. As a result, each is likely to be limited, and it is possible that each has unknown biases. As shown in Figure 2, ITERATE, RAND, and U.S. State Department data show a relatively high correspondence for incident frequency for some years and a low correspondence for others. These differences may be a function of different inclusion rules or simply differences in access to sources. My own review of recent incidents from these

Figure 2. Comparison of ITERATE, RAND, and U.S. State Department counts of terrorist incidents.[26]

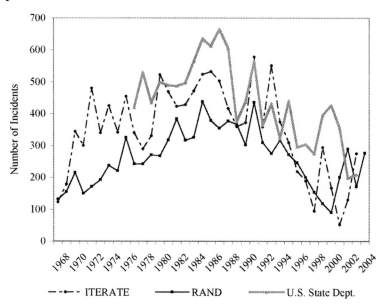

three data sources indicates some differences in inclusion rules. For example, U.S. State Department data include some incidents that are not treated as international or transnational by the other two sources—presumably because they do not involve victims or perpetrators from different countries (e.g., bombings in Kashmir that have no known foreign victims and cannot be attributed to a known group). The RAND database includes Palestinian–Israeli incidents when, for example, Palestinians cross over from the Occupied Territories to Israel to perpetrate a terrorist act. ITER-ATE and State Department data only include such incidents if the victims or perpetrators are from another sovereign state. However, even when similar inclusion/exclusion rules are applied, it is not uncommon for each data set to miss incidents that the others cover.

I chose to use transnational terrorism activity data from more than one data set and combine them into a new data set to be used for the purpose of this project. My primary source of data for transnational terrorist activity is the *International Terrorism: Attributes of Terrorist Events (ITERATE)* data set. However, I supplement this data set with additional data from the *RAND Terrorism Incident Database (RAND–MIPT)*.

I chose to use ITERATE as my primary source for three reasons. First, it is viewed as the most comprehensive data set of transnational terrorist events. Second, it is available both in numeric and in text format. Third, it has been widely used in academic publications. I decided to supplement this data set with data from the RAND–MIPT database because, after comparing the two sets of data, I found that ITERATE misses quite a few incidents that fit its own definition of transnational terrorism, and I believe that merging the data, although following the coding schema of ITERATE, will result in a much richer and more comprehensive set of data.

I decided not to use the State Department data for the following reasons.

First, its definition of international (or transnational) terrorism is more subjective than that of the other two sources. In ITERATE and RAND, transnational or international terrorist incidents are identified only if the perpetrator(s) and victim(s) have different nationalities. This is not the case in the State Department listing, where terrorist incidents are identified as international if they are thought to have international political "ramifications." As a result, incidents that would be coded as domestic and excluded from the transnational data set in ITERATE and RAND are often included in the State Department data.

Second, my own review indicates that it fails to identify incidents that are covered in the other two databases. For example, in the first 2 months of 2003, it fails to identify assassinations or bombings of foreign targets that are identified as transnational terrorist incidents in Turkey, Afghanistan, Bosnia, Pakistan, and Kuwait. Second, where it does identify transnational incidents, it has good overlap with ITERATE. Third, as indicated, it includes many incidents that would be identified as domestic in the other two data sets.

The ITERATE Data Set

The ITERATE data through 1978 are available through the Inter-University Consortium for Political and Social Research (ICPSR) at Ann Arbor, Michigan. The data from 1979 through 2004 are proprietary and available for purchase from Edward Mickolus at Vinyard Software in Dunn Loring, Virginia.

The ITERATE data set is generally considered to be the most comprehensive chronology of international terrorist events that is publicly available and is widely used in academic publications.[27] The data set is based on publicly available news sources[28] and is restricted to international/transnational events.

For the purpose of the data set, ITERATE defines a terrorist event as

> The use, or threat of use, of anxiety-inducing, extra-normal violence for political purposes by any individual or group, whether acting for or in opposition to established governmental authority, when such action is intended to influence the attitudes and behavior of a target group wider than the immediate victims.[29]

This definition differs only slightly from the U.S. Department of State definition of terrorism. For example, ITERATE does not specify that targets must be noncombatant whereas the U.S. State Department does. The State Department definition of non-combatant, however, does not necessarily exclude either military personnel or military bases. ITERATE data are restricted to transnational/international events of terrorism, that is, events "when, through the nationality or foreign ties of its perpetrators, its location, the nature of its institutional or human victims, or the mechanics of its resolution, its ramifications transcend national boundaries."[30]

In ITERATE, domestic incidents of terrorism, that is, incidents that begin and end in the host country and that only have ramifications for that country, are specifically excluded. However, when a terrorist incident in one country involves victims, targets, institutions, or citizens of another country, it is considered transnational or international and is included. The 9/11 hijackings, for example, are included as transnational terrorist incidents for at least three reasons. First, the perpetrators came from outside the United States. Second, the victims were from over 80 countries. And third, the incidents had worldwide economic and security ramifications. The bombings of the U.S. embassies in Kenya and Tanzania on August 7, 1998, as well as the suicide car bombings aimed at British and Jewish targets in Istanbul, Turkey, on November 20, 2003, are similarly included as transnational terrorist incidents since they involve perpetrators and victims from different countries. On the other hand, the bombing of the Murrah Federal Building in Oklahoma City by Timothy McVeigh is not included since it is considered to be a purely domestic event. Similarly, bombings by the IRA in Northern Ireland are not included as transnational terrorist acts. However, IRA attacks in England would be included.

ITERATE makes a distinction between international and transnational terrorism as follows:

> International terrorism is such action when carried out by individuals or groups controlled by a sovereign state, whereas transnational terrorism is carried out by basically autonomous nonstate actors whether or not they enjoy some degree of support from sympathetic states.

Overall, ITERATE, which is available in text and numeric formats, provides a rich events data set of more than 13,000 incidents of transnational terrorism across 192 countries (as well as international organizations such as the UN) from 1968 through 2004.

The RAND–MIPT Data Set

The RAND–MIPT Terrorism Incident Database (1968–2005) is an extension of the RAND Chronology of International Terrorism, which covers incidents of international/transnational terrorism for the period 1968 to 1998. It is available on the Web from the Oklahoma City National Memorial Institute for the Prevention of Terrorism at http://www.tkb.org./Home.jsp.

The RAND database, which includes approximately 10,000 incidents of international/transnational terrorism for the period from 1968 to 2004, was originally developed as an "uncoded textual chronology" of significant international terrorist incidents. Among the RAND terrorism analysts who have contributed to the RAND Chronology over time are terrorism experts such as Brian Jenkins, Bruce Hoffman, and more recently Michael Wermuth and Kim Cragin.

Like ITERATE, the RAND database is based primarily on publicly available news service sources. According to a personal communication from RAND, these news service sources are monitored by regional specialists with travel experience and language expertise. RAND also makes use of government reports. For the period 1968 to 1997, the RAND data set is restricted to international/transnational terrorist incidents. However, the RAND database provides a separate listing of domestic and international/transnational events for the period 1998 to 2004.

Definitions

RAND's definition of a terrorist event is similar to that of ITERATE:

> Terrorism is violence calculated to create an atmosphere of fear and alarm to coerce others into actions they would not otherwise undertake, or refrain from actions they desired to take. Acts of terrorism are generally directed against civilian targets. The motives of all terrorists are political, and terrorist actions are generally carried out in a way that will achieve maximum publicity.[31]

RAND'S definition of international/transnational incidents is also similar. International/transnational incidents are defined as "incidents in which the perpetrators go abroad to strike their targets, select domestic targets associated with a foreign state, or create an international incident by attacking airline passengers or equipment." Domestic terrorist incidents are similarly defined, in this case as incidents perpetrated by local nationals against a purely domestic target.[32]

Similarities and Differences in Sources

The ITERATE and the RAND data sets both exclude the following:

- Incidents that are strictly criminal (e.g., drug trafficking) even if carried out by an identifiable terrorist organization
- Incidents associated with guerrilla attacks on military targets of an occupying force
- Incidents considered to be unintended; for example, when a tourist is killed in the crossfire between a host military and guerillas
- General rioting and protest
- Unsubstantiated threats

- Official government acts in response to terrorist attacks such as the U.S. bombing of Libya, its bombings in Afghanistan and Iraq, or targeted assassinations by the government of Israel

The main differences in terms of inclusion/exclusion rules between the two data sets are threefold. First, RAND includes attacks by Palestinians (in the Occupied Territories) on Israeli civilian targets and attacks by Israelis on Palestinian targets (in the Occupied Territories). ITERATE only includes such attacks if foreigners are harmed. Second, RAND excludes terrorist incidents that are officially sanctioned by governments. ITERATE includes a small number of incidents in which governments are known to have provided direct support or there is officially sanctioned government participation. Such incidents account for less than 1% of the data set. Third, RAND excludes incidents that are aborted by terrorists or stopped by authorities at or before initiation although such incidents are counted in ITERATE.

The two sources also differ in the number of variables they code and in coding schema. ITERATE's numeric data set contains 43 variables grouped into four broad categories. They include:

- Incident characteristics including the date, location, and type of each event (e.g., skyjacking, bombing, kidnapping, barricade/hostage), whether it is state sponsored, and the number of nationalities involved
- Terrorist characteristics including the number, their national origins, and the names (where known) of groups involved in the incident
- Victim characteristics including the nature, number, and national origins of the victims involved in the incident

- Life and property losses that quantify damage in terms of numbers and types of individuals wounded or killed in the incident and give estimates in dollars of property damages

Additional data are provided on the type of weapon used in the incident and whether it was a logistical success (e.g., aborted before initiation, stopped by authorities, or apparently completed as planned).

Although the RAND database provides textual information for the same categories, it only codes the following variables: source of information for incident (e.g., media source and date of publication), date of incident, identity of terrorist group if known, site of incident, number of fatalities, number of injuries, type of weapon, target (e.g., diplomatic, private property or citizens, NGO), whether the attack was state sponsored, and whether it was claimed. However, since RAND provides a textual description of each incident, I was able to recode the data following the ITERATE format.

STATISTICAL APPROACH

A basic assumption behind the use of the two databases (ITERATE and RAND) was that a richer, more comprehensive data set would be obtained. Before merging incident data from the two data sets and eliminating duplicate incidents,[33] I examined the distributions of the main dependent variables in each data set. To test the assumption, I also compared the means and frequency distributions of the main outcome measures across the two databases. In these comparisons, performed with JMP 5.1 statistical software, I used independent *t*-tests and ANOVAs for numeric variables and chi-square for categorical variables.[34] After merging the data sets and eliminating duplicates, I also used JMP statistical software to compare the means and frequency distributions of unique and overlapping (duplicate) incidents in the merged data set. In addition, I used JMP for descriptive statistics to characterize the main outcome measures in the merged data set.[35]

> Everything should be made as simple as possible, but not simpler.
>
> —Albert Einstein

A variety of statistical methods could be applied to test the empirical hypotheses set out in this study. They range from simple (before-after comparisons) to more sophisticated (multiple regression) and more complex (autoregressive-integrated moving average, ARIMA) models. Comparative studies of statistical methods, however, have found that, in most cases, ARIMA models provide more accurate accounting for regularities in time series data than do alternative strategies of analysis, such as before-after comparisons and regression.[36]

Cook and Campbell contend that statistical methods using ordinary least squares methods are not the best approach for interrupted or intervention time series designs since these methods assume independence of errors, an assumption that cannot be made when events or behaviors are measured over time.[37] They recommend using ARIMA models (developed by Box and Jenkins, 1976), since these models are designed to provide unbiased estimates of the error in a series. In these models, the "noise" in a series is modeled. The intervention component is then added to the model. The next step is to determine whether the intervention adds significantly to predicting the behavior of a time series over and above the prediction derived from understanding the regular and seasonal components of the noise. As a rule, ARIMA models require at least 20 observation points preintervention.[38]

This approach is particularly suited to identifying significant shifts in time series associated with interventions. Time series analyses have been used by Midlarsky Crenshaw and Yohida to examine why terrorism spreads; by Brophy-Bearmann and Conybeare to investigate the impact of retaliatory raids on terrorism in Israel; by Enders and Sandler to assess the effects of antiterrorist policies; by O'Brien to examine linkages between foreign policy crises and terrorism; by Weimann and Bernd Brosius to predict who might be victims of terrorist acts; and by Willer to examine the effects of government-issued terror ratings on presidential approval ratings.[39]

Rock, who used the ARIMA model to investigate the impact of changes in speed limits on road accidents, deaths, and injuries, points out that the ARIMA technique is unique in that it is not arbitrarily fitted to data, but is built empirically. The goal is to describe the autocorrelation structure of the series and filter out any variance in the dependent variable (e.g., number of deaths from terrorist acts) that is "predictable on the basis of the past history of the variable." The first step is to build a model of the preintervention data. This step involves displaying the autocorrelation and partial autocorrelation functions (ACF, PACF).

> From these, a preliminary model is identified, indicating the nature of up to three filters that may need to be applied to the raw data. If secular trends in the data are evident, the first filter will be used to account for them. The coefficients for the parameters of the autoregressive and/or moving average filters, if needed, are next estimated. Using diagnostic tests (including the statistical significance of the parameters, the residual ACF and PACF, the Box-Ljung Q statistic, and the Akaike information criterion) the model is critiqued and re-identified, if necessary. If the variance of the data changes over time, a logarithmic or other transformation is applied. The raw data are then passed through the specified filters. Remaining changes in the data can be related to the effects of an intervention term that began at a specified time (such as

> a change in policy or the onset of an intervention); the value and statistical significance of this term will indicate to what extent the policy had an impact.[40]

ARIMA has additional advantages. As Rock observes, it takes into account all the significant autocorrelations within each variable and does not simply assume that the error terms are independent (as regression does) or only characterized by first-order autoregression. This means that any regular pattern over time in the dependent variable is not considered as a possible causal effect between the variables. Such intraseries regularities are filtered out first. Moreover, the effects of exogenous variables can be controlled, independent error terms are obtained, and these procedures are a conservative test of the causal connection between two variables.[41]

After extracting quarterly time series for the tests of my hypotheses, I employed Eviews 4.1 statistical software for the analysis.[42] I began by running a time series least squares regression to examine the preintervention data over time for each of the outcome variables.

One basic assumption of least squares regression is that a series is randomly drawn from a normal distribution with zero mean and constant variance; that is, a white noise process.[43] When this assumption of normality is not met, variable transformation may be necessary.[44] With the exception of all variables constructed as percentages, it was clear from the examination of the Eviews output that the normality assumption was not met and log transformation of these variables was performed.

An assumption of ARIMA modeling is that a series is stationary. To assess stationarity, the residuals (forecasting errors)[45] need to be examined for potential autocorrelation. Autocorrelation occurs when current values are affected by past values (e.g., a high population density on Day 7 is associated with a high population density on Day 6, or a high number of terrorist incidents in one quarter is associated with a high number in the next quarter). Autocorrelation needs to be addressed in time series because it can lead to inefficient estimates of correlation coefficients, underestimation of error terms, and difficulty using standard procedures including *t*-tests and *F*-tests.[46] The main test used to detect autocorrelation is the Durbin–Watson test.[47]

Using the Durbin–Watson test, I found significant autocorrelation in all the time series I extracted.[48] To correct for this problem, I elected to build ARIMA models (for each series) to take out autocorrelation. The choice of model was based on Eviews recommendations:

> The next step is to decide what kind of ARIMA model to use. If the autocorrelation function dies off smoothly at a geometric rate, and the partial autocorrelations were zero after one lag, then a first-order autoregressive model would be suggested. Alternatively, if the autocorrelations were zero after one lag and the partial autocorrelations declined geometrically, a first-order moving average process would come to mind.[49]

Eviews estimates ARIMA models using conditional maximum likelihood estimation. It is possible to include as many moving average (MA) and autogregressive average (AR) terms as you like in the equation. The goal, however, is a "parsimonious representation of the process, i.e. using only enough AR and MA terms to fit the properties of the residuals."[50]

In most cases, I found an AR(2) model (second order autoregressive model) to work best. Once the autocorrelation was specified, errors were again evaluated to ensure a white noise process. When the series appeared stationary and autocorrelation coefficients were not significantly different from 0 (i.e., the series could be considered to be white noise), I concluded that the model was correctly specified.

Having chosen the model, I proceeded to the next step. Since the research was focused on the specific effects of a known intervention (the onset of the War on Terrorism) and other events (the War in Iraq, the capture of Saddam Hussein, and the release of photos from Abu Ghraib), all occurring in the time period of interest, I adapted the ARIMA model to include these interventions. The timing of the onset of the War on Terrorism and the other events were each represented as binary or dummy variables (with "0" values for before the intervention/event and "1" values during and after the intervention/event).[51] As such, they each represented independent or predictor variables.[52]

After running the time series regression, I examined the percentage of variation (R-square) explained by the combination of time and the intervention variables, and I examined the F-statistic to see if it was statistically significant. I also examined the Durbin–Watson statistic to ensure that it was close to two and no significant autocorrelation was observed. In addition, I examined the goodness of fit of the model (e.g., the Akaike information criteria).

I then examined the extent to which time and each of the other predictor variables were significantly associated with the outcome measure (t-statistics) and examined each of their coefficients to determine how much, if at all, they shifted the time series positively or negatively when the other predictor variables were held steady. For log-transformed variables, the coefficients represented the percentage change (positive or negative) from the quarterly average (for the full period before the intervention took place). For non-log transformed variables (i.e., all percentage variables), the coefficients represented the quarterly unit change that, in this case, was equivalent to the percentage change from the quarterly average before the intervention took place. In some cases, high coefficients were less significant (had higher probability or p-values) than coefficients that were lower. This outcome was most likely a function of the amount of variance in the apparent effect of the event. Put simply, events that were associated with consistent change from quarter to quarter were likely to have lower (more significant) *p*-values regardless of the amount of change they appeared to produce.

LIMITATIONS

All research designs have limitations. Two considerations relating to the design and analysis of this study are reliability and validity.

Reliability

Reliability refers to the stability or consistency with which measurements are made. If measurements are not made reliably, there is a potential for validity to be threatened. Unreliability may occur as a result of error or systematic bias. As Cook and Campbell point out, "most data used in time series come from archives." As a result, the data need to be carefully examined for systematic bias.[53] In this study, in which the database is derived from data sets based on media sources, there is a potential for error when incidents are missed and not recorded or when incidents are systematically excluded because they are not covered in major news media used to construct the database. In addition, what is considered newsworthy may change over time and coding of incidents may change as those entering the data became aware of a problem in the data.

In relation to terrorism incident data, Mickolus points out that an events approach also "depends on the inter-coder reliability of the research team." He goes on to observe:

> The principal investigator must constantly be on the alert to tiny differences in the understanding of coders regarding what each of the variables and their values measure.

> Tests must be taken from time to time to ensure that small
> biases are not being introduced to the dataset by simple
> errors, errors in sources, misunderstanding, coder support
> for the underlying causes of groups, and the like.[54]

All coding rules should be prespecified and documented in a codebook and extensive training is necessary especially when there are changes in coders. Arbitrary cases need to be discussed and such discussions may lead to new rules or greater specification of existing ones.[55] In addition, as Koopman and Rucht, in relation to protest events, point out,

> Intra- and inter-reliability tests of all coders should be
> carried out to identify and document reliability both for
> the primary selection (to which degree are candidate
> articles retrieved and events contained in them identified)
> and for the secondary selection of categories within key
> variables.[56]

Most experts advise that reliability tests be conducted not only at the beginning of data collection but also at regular intervals during the process of data entry. Such comparisons allow one to identify flaws, errors, and misinterpretation of coding rules.

A reliability strength of ITERATE is that it has been maintained for its lifetime by one person, Edward Mickolus. In addition, all entries into the numeric database follow explicit rules set out in a codebook and are cross-linked by a code number to a textual database, which gives the date and media source, as well as a textual summary. RAND–MIPT incident codes are also cross-linked to textual data that provide the date and media source. All are channeled through terrorism specialists at RAND, questionable incidents are reviewed by a joint vetting committee of MIPT and RAND staff and, according to a RAND–MIPT source, all are selected in a accordance with the original Chronology's long standing definition to ensure consistence and accuracy. Moreover, they usually have two or more sources, the number of people who have worked on the databases over the last few decades has been small, all incidents are reviewed by at least two people, and users of the RAND Web site are encouraged to provide feedback and suggest incidents that may have been omitted.[57] Still, the cautions outlined previously need to be taken into consideration. Although both databases have taken steps to ensure reliability, the absence of published data on the intra- and intercoder reliabilities of each of these databases is a weakness.

To maintain coding consistency between the two databases, I used ITERATE's Coding Book to code RAND text-based incidents.[58] Coding questions that I could not answer using the ITERATE Code Book was resolved by consulting textual descriptions of duplicate events and how they were coded in ITERATE. I also developed coding criteria for each of the variables I recoded for the purpose of the study. These criteria, together with the original ITERATE codes used here, are discussed in chapter 6 in the context of overall results.

Validity

Validity refers to the accuracy of a result. Does it capture the actual state of affairs? And how well can it be extended to other contexts or times?[59] Two concerns in this study are internal validity and external validity, that is, generalizability.[60]

When a causal relationship between an intervention and an outcome is found, it is said to have *internal validity*. The internal validity of a study, however, may be threatened in a variety of ways. The interrupted time series design used here generally pro-tects against two major threats to validity—namely, *maturation* and *regression to the mean*—by considering multiple observations before and after an intervention. This design, however, is subject to other threats.

One such threat is *history* (i.e., the occurrence of things other than the intervention that might affect the dependent variable). It is possible that the occurrence of events other than those studied here could have influenced or confounded the results. Such events might include economic or social changes occurring independently of the War on Terrorism or mediated by that campaign. They might also include natural disasters, such as the December 26, 2004, tsunami, which could affect the availability of resources for individuals or groups to carry out terrorism or conversely the availability of resources for counterterrorism efforts in the following period. The argument could even be made that a watermark event such as 9/11, which directly preceded the onset of the War on Terrorism, was more important than the war itself in mobilizing subsequent transnational terrorism. It could also be argued that the release of photos of abuse from Abu Ghraib was not as important as the siege of Fallujah, an event that also occurred in April 2004.

A second threat is *selection bias*, which could have occurred, as previously noted, if some incidents were systematically excluded. As has been stressed, the data sets are limited to *newsworthy* incidents, that is, ones that are covered in major news service sources. It is possible that incidents that meet the specified criteria for transnational terrorism are not reported because they were not considered newsworthy or because they occurred in totalitarian states that keep a tight control over news services.

A third potential threat is *instrumentation* bias; for example, if there were changes in the way records of incidents were kept in the sources used over the time period used. In general, I have been reassured that the instruments have been kept in a way that is consistent. Nonetheless, such biases may have crept in.

A fourth threat in the design used is that posed by an intervention only gradually diffusing through the population or having delayed effects. In relation to *diffusion*, it could be argued that the

War on Terrorism has diffused differentially. Its impact may be stronger in some regions, for example, the Middle East and South Asia, than in others, for example, Africa and South America. Even within these regions, it is likely to be having more effect in countries where "boots are on the ground" as opposed to countries where they are not. To test this possibility in a limited way, I have examined the dispersion of transnational incidents in three ways: across countries, across the Muslim world (defined as countries with at least 50% Muslims), and across regions. However, it is also possible that it is too early to measure the true impact of the GWOT or the other predictor variables because these events may have delayed effects that cannot be captured at this point in time.

Finally, there is the problem of the absence of counterfactuals. Historical data cannot be manipulated as might occur in a strict experimental design. This means, in this case, that the design cannot control for what might have happened had there never been a War on Terrorism. The absence of this counterfactual poses another problem for inference. As Stern and Druckman observe:

> To support a conclusion that an intervention had a particular effect requires answering the following question: What would have happened if the intervention had not been tried when it was? It implies a comparison between what actually happened after the intervention and alternative histories in which the intervention was not tried, or was tried earlier or later in the conflict, or a different intervention was tried. This involves comparisons with hypothetical or counterfactual worlds, which history does not provide.[61]

Although this is a limitation of the design, patterns that emerge here may provide useful material for future research based on other methods, for example, process tracing,[62] simulation,[63] and intensive study of individual cases over time.[64]

Although time series designs are thought to be strong in controlling for threats to *external validity*, the generalizability of the study is still limited for several reasons. First, I focus exclusively on transnational terrorist incidents carried out by substate or nonstate groups or individuals. The results cannot, therefore, be generalized to domestic terrorist incidents or incidents perpetrated by other entities (e.g., states). Second, I focus on incidents in quarterly periods. As a result, generalizations cannot be made to other calendar periods (days, months, years). Third, I restrict the analysis of deadly incidents to the number of incidents with deaths. This means that shifts in these incidents cannot be extrapolated to mean that overall casualties have increased or decreased. An increase, for example, in deadly incidents does not necessarily mean that more people have died from these incidents. Finally, it needs to be cautioned that the War on Terrorism has encompassed many elements beyond military force. For example, it also has police, intelligence, and diplomatic elements. Given the design, it is not possible to determine which elements are absolutely responsible for a given effect.

> All models are wrong; some models are useful.
>
> —George Box

Other Qualifications

As George Box points out, no model is perfect although some are more useful than others. Several qualifications need to be addressed regarding the technique used here.

First, like other models such as regression, ARIMA is sensitive to outliers in the data. This is of particular concern with fatality and frequency data since such data tend not to be normally distributed. For this reason, I had to log transform several of the time series before fitting an ARIMA model.

Second, the choice of an ARIMA formulation may be viewed as subjective. Often, multiple formulations are found to be adequate. For this reason, I employed diagnostic checking including residual diagnostics (e.g., autocorrelations and partial autocorrelations) and goodness-of-fit checks (e.g., the Akaike information criteria).

Third, in the analysis of the impact of the War on Terrorism, I used a step intervention approach. This approach is limited to an examination of *permanent* shifts in the means of the variables tested. However, other patterns of intervention beyond an abrupt, permanent one could be examined. For example, it might be considered by some to be more appropriate in reference to the War in Iraq to use a two-step process beginning with a period of anticipation when the possibility of war was being debated in late 2002 and then implemented in 2003.

Fourth, a properly modeled ARIMA should account for clear trends in the data from confounding variables such as the influence of other variables. In this study, the focus is on the impact of the War on Terrorism with its emphasis on preemptive force and three other predictor variables. However, changes in intelligence gathering, increases in intercountry cooperation on terrorism, and changes in the ability of countries to cut off terrorist financing may also be important but could not be captured in this analysis since much of this information is classified.

Finally, the number of observations or data points may limit my ability to establish statistical trends. Statistical analysis of time series theoretically require over 50 observations and preferably over 100 observations.[65] For theoretical reasons relating to the rise of terrorist activity by Islamist organizations and for Islamist causes, I have chosen to limit the preintervention period to data beginning in 1993. Although I will only have 48 observations, I have been advised that this number should be sufficient.[66]

All research designs have limitations. One approach to resolving these limitations is to adopt a strategy of "triangulation."[67] The underlying assumption behind this strategy is that "multiple perspectives, sources of data, constructs, interpretive frameworks, and modes of analysis" are an improvement over any single approach and engender more confidence when they converge on the same findings.[68] In this study, I address some of the previously described reliability and validity limitations by using more than one source of data (ITERATE and RAND), more than one measure of terrorism, and a number of interpretive frameworks (rational choice theory, resource mobilization theory, asymmetric war theory, conflict resolution theory). Future studies, adopting other perspectives, other constructs, sources of data, and other frameworks and methods will undoubtedly build on the results presented here.

CHAPTER 6

ARE WE WINNING? THE RESULTS

With many calculations, one can win; with few one cannot. How much less chance of victory has one who makes none at all!

—Sun Tzu

I can think of nothing more gallant, even though again and again we fail, than attempting to get at the facts; attempting to tell things as they really are. For at least reality, though never fully attained, can be defined. Reality is that which, when you don't believe in it, doesn't go away.

—Peter Viereck[1]

Never argue. In society nothing must be discussed; give only results.

—Benjamin Disraeli

For the 12-year study period 1993 to 2004, the combined number of transnational terrorist incidents in ITERATE and RAND was

5,596. Of these, 863 incidents (30% in ITERATE and 32% in RAND) proved to be duplicates; that is, descriptions of the same incidents occurring on the same day in the same location. I decided that an incident was a duplicate if it was reported, in both incidents, to have occurred on the same day, in the same locale, and if the textual description matched on most details (type of attack, number of victims, alleged perpetrators, deaths, injuries). In a few cases, a spate of attacks (e.g., several bombings in a capital city) that matched on other details was counted differently; that is, as one incident in one database and as three incidents in the other database. In these instances, I counted the incident three times rather than once. In a few cases, it was not possible to determine if an incident was a duplicate since not enough detail was provided. For example, ITERATE reported as many as 75 bombing incidents against U.S. targets in Colombia in one month in 1999 but did not give the daily dates of these attacks. In this case, since RAND reported a smaller number of similar incidents in Colombia during the same period, I counted this smaller number of incidents as duplicates.

Before merging the data and eliminating duplicates, I compared the two databases (ITERATE and RAND) to see how well they corresponded on the main outcome measures. These preliminary analyses showed that, taken separately, ITERATE and RAND tapped into somewhat different locations, types of incidents, and types of victims. As such, the analyses supported my strategy of using two databases to obtain a richer and more comprehensive data set. After merging the data, I examined the overall characteristics of incidents in the merged data set. In addition, since overlapping incidents may provide clues to a core of agreement on terrorist incidents, I made several comparisons between overlapping and unique incidents. I then proceeded to run the time series regression analyses to test the hypotheses outlined in chapter 5. The results of these analyses are presented next.

The final merged data set contained a total of 4,733 transnational incidents. Of these, 42% were exclusively from ITERATE, 40% were exclusively from RAND, and 18% represented overlapping incidents, that is, incidents present in both sources (Figure 3).

THE BIRD'S-EYE VIEW

The average number of incidents per quarterly (3 months) period was 98.6 ± 45.6 (range 35–271 per quarter) for the combined data set over the period 1993 to 2004.

Since both databases listed each incident by country of occurrence, it was possible to categorize incidents by region of occurrence using the seven-region World Bank classification.

The largest concentration of attacks (32%) for the study period was in Europe and Central Asia. However, the Middle East and North Africa had almost as large a share of attacks (29%). In contrast, the Sub-Saharan Africa region had only a third as many attacks whereas Latin America had half as many. Although the North American

Figure 3. Percent distribution of transnational terrorist incidents by source, 1993–2004.

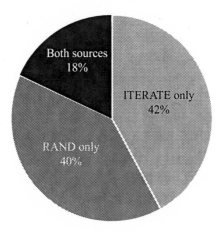

Figure 4. Percent distribution of transnational terrorist incidents by World Bank Region, 1993–2004.

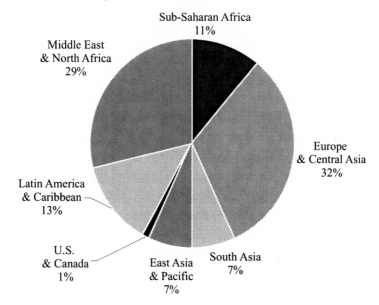

region, because of September 11, suffered more casualties than any other region, it accounted for only 1% of the all incidents (Figure 4).[2]

To assess the daily frequency of transnational terrorist activity, I summed the number of quarterly days on which at least one incident occurred during the study period.[3] As shown in the following, the mean number of days of transnational terrorist activity per quarter (3-month, or approximately 90 days, period) was 52.5 ± 13.4 days (range 30–82 days). In other words, transnational terrorist activity was observed on average on 58% of the available days each quarter (Figure 5).

Analysis of the country distribution of incidents indicated that transnational terrorist incidents were reported in 160 named countries or disputed territories.[4] Of these, 24 countries or territories were identified as having 50 or more transnational terrorist incidents

Figure 5. Mean number of quarterly days of transnational terrorist activity, 1993–2004.

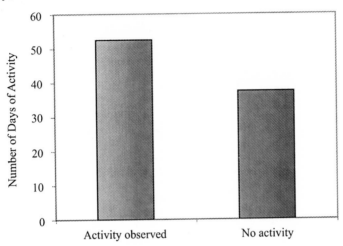

within their borders and accounted for 69% of all incidents over the study period.

As shown in Figure 6, four countries (Israel, Iraq, Colombia, and Greece) each had more than 300 incidents over the study period. Within the Middle East and North African region, the largest concentrations of attacks were in Israel, Iraq, Somalia, Turkey, Yemen, and Algeria.

In South Asia, the countries with the largest contributions were Pakistan, Afghanistan, and India. (The relative contributions of these countries may have been lower than in U.S. State Department data because the latter data set counts incidents considered to have international or transnational "ramifications" or to be "significant" to the U.S. even if transnationality in the form of perpetrators and victims being from different countries is not strictly found.)

Attacks in Germany, Greece, the United Kingdom, and France dominated the regional profile in Europe, whereas attacks in

Figure 6. Number of transnational terrorist incidents in countries with 50+ incidents, 1993–2004.

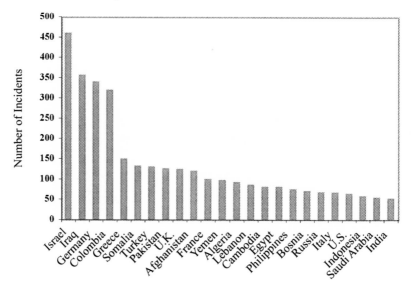

Colombia and Peru were the most dominant in terms of number for the Latin American region.

I also examined the distribution of incidents in countries with populations classified as having 50% or more Muslim populations. Forty-one such countries were identified. Transnational terrorist attacks within the borders of these countries constituted 36% of all incidents in the merged database.

Both sources identified the type of attack for each incident. However, ITERATE used a more detailed system of classification than RAND. For the overall classification, I used ITER-ATE's classification system to code textual data in RAND. Using this classification, I found that the most common type of attack was bombing. As shown in Figure 7, explosive bombings consti-tuted 21% of all attacks, whereas fire and fire bombings made up 10%. Armed attacks, with rifles, machine guns, and other armed

Figure 7. Percent distribution of transnational terrorist incidents, by type of attack, 1993–2004.

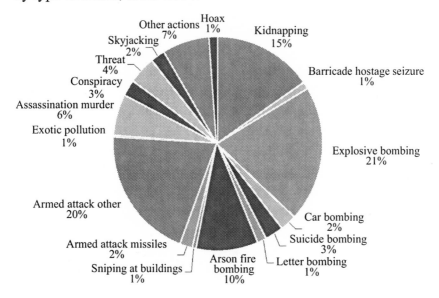

weapons, were the next most frequent type of attack, accounting for 20% of all attacks, and kidnappings (hostage seizures) were the next most frequent at 15%. On the other hand, skyjackings and barricade hostage seizures comprised very small proportions of all incidents, 2% and 1%, respectively.[5]

Note: "Other" includes takeover of trains and buses (13 incidents), occupation of facilities (11 incidents), arms smuggling (8 incidents), shoot-out with police (8 incidents), theft and break-in (18 incidents), sabotage (6 incidents), unknown (7 incidents), and other miscellaneous actions including stabbings and attacks with sharp objects (272 incidents). Fifteen incidents, characterized as chemical biological (or exotic pollution) constituted less than 1% of all incidents.

Both databases coded the number of deaths and the number of injuries associated with an incident, if any, if known. In several cases, the databases differed on the actual number of dead or injured for the same incident. This occurred most frequently for large events (such as 9/11, the 1998 embassy bombings in Kenya, and the August 8, 2001, attack in Israel) when ITERATE listed the number of dead as unknown whereas RAND gave exact numbers based on a cited news source. I classified incidents as deadly if one or more deaths were reported in either database for an incident or if the incident was associated in either database with deaths in the textual description—even if the exact number was unknown.[6]

The majority of attacks were not associated with deaths or injuries. Deadly attacks made up only 27% of all attacks in the combined data set (Figure 8). Of these, approximately 42% involved 1 death, 31% involved 2 to 5 deaths, 15% involved 6 to 20 deaths, and 4% involved 21 to 100 deaths. Less than 1% of all incidents involved more than 100 deaths, and in 7% the number of deaths was unknown. Twenty-four percent of the attacks could be identi-

Figure 8. Percent distribution of transnational terrorist incidents by lethality, 1993–2004.

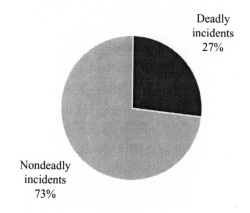

fied as being associated with injuries only (no deaths) and 38% with injuries, deaths, or a combination of both.[7]

The two databases used slightly different systems for classifying the victims of attacks. ITERATE classified the "type of immediate victim," whereas RAND classified the "target" of attack. This difference led to some discrepancies, for example, when the target of an attack was the foreign military but the immediate victim was a private citizen. As discussed earlier in Methods, I used RAND's textual description to code the type of immediate victim following ITERATE.

In 39% of the incidents, the immediate victim was a private citizen or party. Lower proportions of incidents (21% and 18%) involved businesses (persons and or property) and foreign diplomats (including embassy personnel and property, as well as other foreign government officials). Attacks on military (foreign or domestic) were not counted in either database unless those attacks represented attacks when the military were at rest (as in the U.S.S. Cole attack) or the attack involved private citizens, as well as military. As a result, such attacks made up relatively small proportions of the data set (Figure 9).

Both databases supplied the nationality of the victims when the information was available. I coded the victim as multinational if ITERATE or RAND reported more than one nationality among victims, or coded the victim as an international organization such as the UN or Red Cross. Using this system, about one third of all incidents could be identified as involving a multinational victim. Such incidents included not only situations such as an attack on a café frequented by locals and foreigners in Israel but also incidents in which an international organization (such as the Red Cross or UNICEF) or its members were the victims (Figure 10).

ITERATE specifically coded the number, if any, of U.S. victims and the type of U.S. victim. I used ITERATE's system to code the presence of U.S. victims in RAND's data. Using this system, 25%

Figure 9. Percent distribution of transnational terrorist incidents by type of immediate victim, 1993–2004.

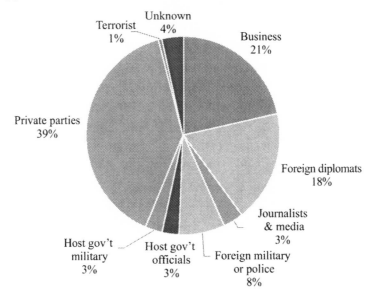

Figure 10. Percent distribution of transnational terrorist incidents by multinational victims, 1993–2004.

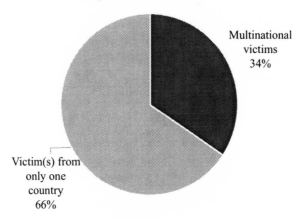

of all incidents could be identified as involving one or more U.S. victims. (Some of these incidents involved victims of other countries, e.g., when an attack on a U.S. embassy injured local, as well as U.S. citizens.) Of the attacks that could be classified as involving a U.S. victim, 38% involved U.S. business officials or business property as an immediate victim and 27% involved parties; for example, missionaries, tourists, students, or representatives of NGOs. A smaller proportion (21%) involved diplomatic personnel or property (Figure 11).[8]

Both databases identified the perpetrator group where known. In more than 50% of the incidents, no perpetrator group or organization was identified by name. For the remaining attacks, that is, those that were identified in either database (either because they

Figure 11. Percent distribution of incidents with U.S. victims by type of victim, 1993–2004.

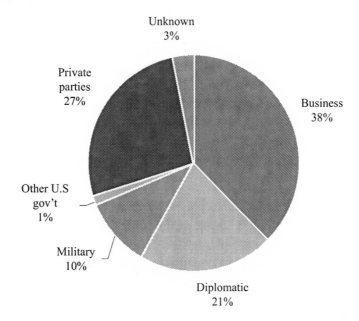

were claimed by an organization or attributed to one), I made the following general classifications.

I included leftist socialist and communist groups such as the Khmer Rouge, Shining Path in Peru, ELN, and FARC, as well as anarchist and antiglobalization groups in a category I called "Leftist, Anarchist, Antiglobalization." I included right-wing extremist and racist groups such as the Neo-Nazis and right-wing Christian, extremist Jewish, and militia groups in a category I called "Right Wing or Racist." I placed secular national separatist groups such as the Irish Republican Army, the Basque Fatherland, the Liberation Tigers of Tamil Eelam (LTTE), and secular Palestinian terrorist guerilla groups, such as Al Fatah and Al Aqsa, in a category called "National Separatist or National Separatist Leftist." Since Islamist extremist violence and so-called Jihadi terrorism have become matters of increasing concern, I placed groups committed to or identified by name or reputation with Islamist causes (e.g., al Qaeda, the Taliban, Jemaah Islamiyah, and the Salafist group) in a separate category. In this category, I also included groups committed to Islamist national separatist causes, for example, the Afghan Mujahideen, Kashmiri rebels, Hezbollah, Hamas, the Palestinian Islamic Jihad (PIJ), Tawid and Jihad, and the Islamic Army in Iraq. Following but adapting RAND's pattern of identifying such groups as "Religious/Religious National Separatist," I named this category "Islamist/Islamist National Separatist."[9] I set aside a separate group called "Government Agents" for a very small number of incidents attributed, mostly in the ITERATE data set, to clandestine agents of governments. Finally, I set up a category called "Other." This category included several groups that did not fit into the other categories; for example, ones identified as Yemeni tribesmen, the West Nile Bank Front, Rwandan rebels, and the RUF in Sierra Leone.[10]

The breakdown of perpetrator groups for the period studied is shown in Figure 12. It should be noted that incidents perpetrated by groups classified as anarchist or antiglobalization made up only a very small percentage (i.e., less than 1%) of the "Leftist, Anarchist, Antiglobalization" group. Similarly, Islamist groups, such as al Qaeda and the Taliban, constituted less than 1% of the category labeled as "Islamist/Islamist National Separatist," whereas groups committed to Islamist *and* national separatist causes comprised more than 99%. Finally, only 22 of the 4,733 incidents were attributed to government agents; for example, alleged Iraqi agents, agents of Turkish Intelligence, and Bahrain government representatives.

SHIFTS IN THE FREQUENCY OF INCIDENTS

My first hypothesis (Hypothesis 1) was that the War on Terrorism has led to an increase in the average quarterly number (frequency) of transnational terrorist incidents. I also hypothesized that

Figure 12. Percent distribution of transnational terrorist incident by type of perpetrator organization, 1993–2004.

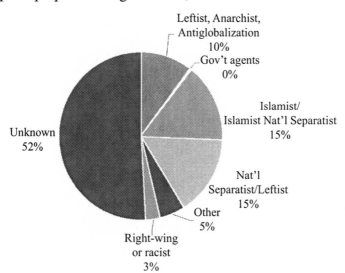

associated events, including the invasion of Iraq, the capture of Saddam Hussein, and the release of photos from Abu Ghraib, would be found to have led to an escalation in the frequency of transnational terrorist incidents (Hypothesis 9).

Figure 13 shows the quarterly time series of transnational terrorist incidents for the merged data set for the 12-year study period. The average quarterly number of incidents before the onset of the War on Terrorism was 97.4 ± 49.2 (range 35–271 per quarter). Visual inspection of this series indicates a pattern of incidents declining after the breakup of the Soviet Union in the early 1990s and rising, albeit with dips, after the onset of the War on Terrorism in October 2003. To what extent was the War on Terrorism and the related events of interest (the invasion of Iraq, the capture of Saddam Hussein, and the release of photos from Abu Ghraib) associated with a shift in this pattern?

Figure 13. Quarterly number of transnational terrorist incidents, 1993–2004.

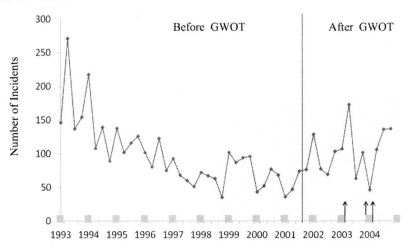

Although time series regression analyses cannot conclusively show causality, the results are compelling.[11] The overall test indicated that a linear trend for time, combined with the GWOT and the other three events (invasion of Iraq, the capture of Saddam Hussein, and the release of photos from Abu Ghraib), did significantly predict the frequency of transnational terrorist incidents over the specified time period ($F = 6.2$; $p = .00007$).[12]

When the other predictor variables were held constant, time was found to have a significant effect ($p > .0001$). In this case, the linear pattern was one of incidents declining on average by 3.3% (or, on average, about three incidents per quarter) over the study period. However, when time and the other predictor variables were held constant, the onset of the War on Terrorism and the release of photos from Abu Ghraib were both found to statistically shift this pattern in the opposite direction.

Specifically, the GWOT was associated with a 74% increase in transnational terrorist incidents ($p = 0.0001$) over and above the period before the GWOT whereas the release of photos from Abu Ghraib was associated with a 110% increase ($p = .0048$) over and above the time period before this event. The invasion of Iraq was also associated with an increase (in this case of 26%) although this increase was not statistically significant. On the other hand, contrary to expectation, the capture of Saddam Hussein was associated with a 77% *decrease* ($p = .049$) in transnational terrorist incidents compared with the full period before the capture. (In raw numbers, this means that compared with the preintervention period, the War on Terrorism added as many as 72 more incidents in a quarter whereas Abu Ghraib added over 100 and the capture of Saddam Hussein reduced the number by about 75 incidents.) These results lend support to Hypothesis 1 but only partial support to Hypothesis 9.

The aforementioned analysis shows that although the War on Terrorism and evidence of abuse at Abu Ghraib were both significantly associated with upward shifts in the number of incidents, and the capture of Saddam Hussein was statistically associated with a downward shift, no statistical effects were found for the invasion of Iraq. A separate analysis, however, showed that when incidents in Israel and the Occupied Territories were excluded from the series, very different results were obtained (Figure 14).

In this analysis, which was significant ($F = 7.5$; $p = .00001$), the linear trend of incidents decreasing by 3% was sustained ($p < .0001$). However, with Israel excluded, neither the GWOT nor the capture of Saddam Hussein was found to have a significant impact on the number of incidents. On the other hand, the invasion of Iraq was found to significantly shift the number of incidents upwards by 66% ($p = .04$) and the release of photos from Abu Ghraib was found to shift the number of incidents upwards by

Figure 14. Quarterly number of transnational terrorist incidents, 1993–2004 (incidents in Israel excluded).

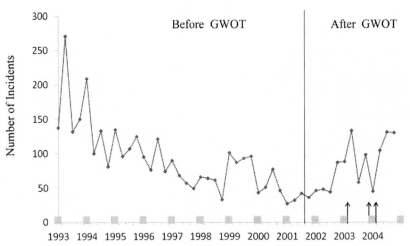

104% ($p = .01$). The discrepancy between this result and the previous one may be a function of the high number of incidents in Israel before the War on Terrorism and the decline in incidents in Israel shortly afterwards. This spike and decline, which is reflected in Figure 13, may have leveled the impact of the invasion of Iraq in the overall analysis. As shown in Figure 14, the removal of incidents from Israel and the Occupied Territories more clearly demonstrates a decline in incidents through the first phase of the GWOT and an increase after the invasion of Iraq in March 2003.

My second hypothesis was that the War on Terrorism would be found to have led to an increase in the number of days on which transnational terrorist incidents occurred (Hypothesis 2). I also hypothesized that associated events including the invasion of Iraq, the capture of Saddam Hussein, and the release of photos from Abu Ghraib would increase the number of days of activity (Hypothesis 9).

Figure 15 displays the time series for the quarterly number of days on which transnational terrorist attacks were observed for the 12-year study period. The average number of days per quarter for the preintervention period was 51.4 ± 13.4 days (range 30–82 days). Visual inspection of the time series for this variable indicates a general pattern of decline in the number of days of activity before the onset of the GWOT and a general pattern of increase afterwards.

In this case, the time series regression for the combined effect of time and the four events of interest was statistically significant ($F = 6.655$; $p = .000023$). As suggested from visual inspection, there was a statistically significant effect for time ($p < .0001$) with the number of days decreasing, on average, by 2% per quarter over the study period. However, significant *increases* in the number of days of activity were associated with the GWOT ($p < .0001$) and the release of photos from Abu Ghraib ($p = .0011$).

Figure 15. Quarterly number of days with transnational terrorist incidents, 1993–2004.

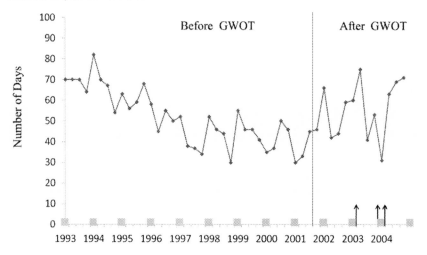

Controlling for time and the other predictor events, the onset of the GWOT was found to increase the quarterly number of days of terrorist activity by 47%, whereas the release of photos from Abu Ghraib was found to increase the number of days of activity by 84%. The invasion of Iraq was also associated with a nonsignificant increase on this measure.[13] On the other hand, when the other events were controlled, the capture of Saddam Hussein was found to be associated with a significant decline by as much as 58% in the number of days of terrorist activity ($p = .02$). In raw numbers, this means that compared with the preintervention period, the War on Terrorism added on average 24 days of activity per quarter, whereas the release of photos from Abu Ghraib added approximately 44 more days, and the capture of Saddam Hussein was associated with a decrease of approximately 30 days. These results lend support to Hypothesis 2 and partial support to Hypothesis 9.

Shifts in the Lethality of Incidents

My third hypothesis was that the onset of the War on Terrorism would be found to have led to an increase in lethal transnational terrorist incidents (Hypothesis 3). I also hypothesized that the invasion of Iraq, the capture of Saddam Hussein, and the release of photos from Abu Ghraib would be associated with increases in lethal incidents (Hypothesis 9).

The average quarterly number of deadly incidents in the preintervention period was 22 ± 11.7 and such incidents made up 27% of all incidents in the merged data set over the study period. To test the extent to which time and the other predictor variables were associated with shifts in the number and percentage of deadly incidents, I extracted a quarterly time series for deadly incidents.

Visual inspection of this series (Figure 16) shows a fluctuating pattern associated with a general pattern of decline in the 1990s and a relatively steep increase in the first years of the millennium.

Figure 16. Quarterly number of deadly transnational terrorist incidents, 1993–2004.

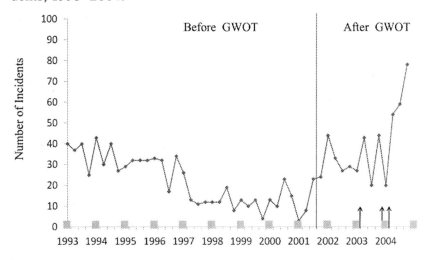

Again, the time series regression was statistically significant ($F = 13.1$; $p = 0000$). In this case, there was a clear linear trend of an almost 6% decrease in deadly events over the study period ($p < .0001$). In raw numbers, this meant that deadly transnational terrorist incidents decreased, on average, by 1.3 incidents per quarter over the study period. However, controlling for time and the other predictor events, the start of the War on Terrorism was associated with a dramatic and significant 168% increase in the number of deadly incidents ($p < .0001$) over and above the preintervention period, whereas the release of photos was associated with a 108% increase (although this finding was significant only at the trend level, $p = .06$). In raw numbers, this meant that the onset of the GWOT added, on average, 37 more deadly incidents per quarter, whereas the release of photos added, on average, 23 more deadly incidents per quarter. These results lend support to Hypothesis 1 and lend partial support to Hypothesis 9.

Was the increase in deadly incidents simply an effect of the increase in the number of incidents? Or did the percentage of all incidents that were deadly also increase after the onset of the War on Terrorism? Visual inspection of Figures 17 and 18 suggests that, as a percentage share, deadly incidents increased after the start of the GWOT.

The time series regression examining the effect of the War on Terrorism and the other variables on deadly incidents, as a percentage of all incidents, was statistically significant ($F = 5.95$; $p = .0001$). In this analysis, no time effect was detected; that is, there was no clear trend of such incidents increasing or decreasing over the study period. Nor was any effect found for the onset of the War in Iraq, the capture of Saddam Hussein, or the release of photos from Abu Ghraib. However, the analysis did indicate that the onset of the GWOT was associated with a significant 16% increase in the percentage of all incidents that were deadly

Figure 17. Deadly transnational terrorist incidents as a percentage of all incidents, 1993–2004.

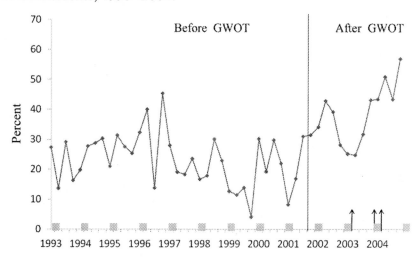

Figure 18. Quarterly percent distribution of deadly and nondeadly transnational terrorist incidents, 1993–2004.

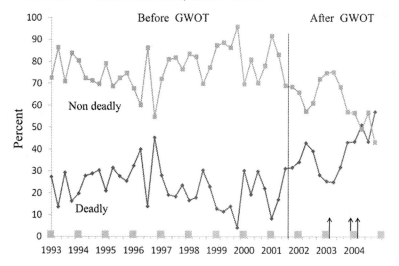

(p = .002). This result suggests that the increase in deadly incidents was not simply a function of the increase in the number of overall incidents but was directly related to the onset of the GWOT.

The results indicate that the onset of the War on Terrorism and to a lesser extent the release of photos from Abu Ghraib were critical variables in the increase in deadly events. However, somewhat different findings were obtained when the analysis of the quarterly series of the number of deadly events was repeated with incidents in Israel and the Occupied Territories excluded. In this analysis (F = 9.5; p = .00001), the effect of the GWOT was still significant (p = .0001), but the release of photos from Abu Ghraib reached statistical significance (p = .017) and the effect of the War in Iraq was also significant (p = .005). Interestingly, the magnitude of the impact of the War on Terrorism was lower when incidents in Israel were excluded (102% vs. 168%), whereas that of the release of photos was higher (140% vs. 108%); the impact of the War in Iraq was statistically significant and almost as large (94%) as that for the GWOT. These results suggest that the War in Iraq *was* critical in the rise in the number of deadly transnational terrorist incidents outside of Israel.

Because of the skewness of the data, I did not apply time series analysis to examine shifts in the number of deaths (individuals killed) associated with transnational terrorist incidents. However, I did look at the overall pattern of change. As shown in Figure 19, the attacks that took place on September 11, 2001, represented a watershed. The median number of deaths in the 8½-year period before 9/11 was 92.5. On September 11, 2001, more than 3,000 people were killed. No such incident has occurred since the start of the War on Terrorism. However, the quarterly number of deaths associated with transnational terrorism was greater after the start of the GWOT than it was before September 11, 2001.

Figure 19. Quarterly number of deaths from transnational terrorist incidents, 1993–2004.

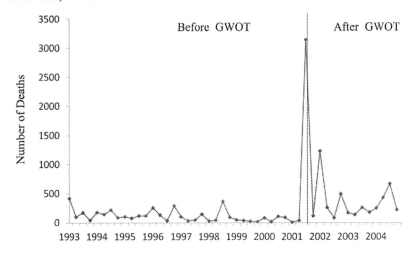

In the 3½-year period after the start of the War on Terrorism, the median quarterly number of deaths rose to 248. After the invasion of Iraq, the median number was 253, and after Abu Ghraib it was as high as 431.

I did apply time series analysis to examine the pattern of change in the number of incidents with deaths *or* injuries. The average number of such incidents was 33 ± 18.2 in the preintervention period. The pattern of change here (Figure 20) was somewhat clearer than that for deadly incidents but the regression results were similar.

In this analysis, which was significant ($F = 13.4$; $p < .0001$), the regression showed a significant linear trend of incidents with deaths or injuries decreasing, on average, by 1.2 incidents per quarter over the time period ($p = .0026$). Again, the results indicated that this pattern was significantly shifted in the opposite direction after the onset of the War on Terrorism ($p = .0047$) and after the

Figure 20. Number of transnational terrorist incidents with deaths or injuries, 1993–2004.

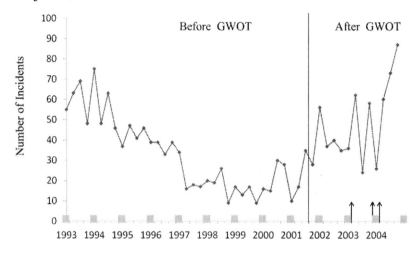

release of photos from Abu Ghraib ($p = .002$). However, in this case, the number of incidents with deaths or injuries showed a trend ($p < .08$) toward an increase in relation to the onset of the War in Iraq. In raw numbers, the onset of the War on Terrorism was found to increase such incidents by an average of 28.6 incidents per quarter over the preintervention average, the invasion of Iraq by 15.7 incidents per quarter, and the release of photos from Abu Ghraib by a dramatic 41.1 incidents per quarter.

When the same analysis was run with incidents in Israel excluded, similar results were found. In this analysis ($F = 7.6$; $p = .000004$), the largest effect was for Abu Ghraib, raising such incidents by 115% ($p = .029$). The second largest effect was for the invasion of Iraq, raising such incidents by 93% ($p = .0046$), and the third largest effect was for the onset of the GWOT, which was associated with a 73% increase ($p = .0039$).

SHIFTS IN THE DISPERSION AND LOCATION OF INCIDENTS

My fourth hypothesis was that the War on Terrorism would be found to have led to an increase in the dispersion of transnational terrorism. I hypothesized that it would be associated, in particular, with an increased number of places (countries) where transnational terrorism occurred (Hypothesis 4a). In addition, I hypothesized that the other events (invasion of Iraq, capture of Saddam Hussein, and release of photos from Abu Ghraib) would increase dispersion (Hypothesis 9).

The average quarterly number of countries with transnational terrorist activity (incidents) before the War on Terrorism was 36.6 ± 9.9 (range 21–54 countries). Visual inspection of the time series (Figure 21) shows a pattern of decline from the early until the mid-1990s and a series of spikes thereafter. The time series regression, which was statistically significant ($F = 11.71; p < .0001$) demonstrated a linear decline, on average, of 2.5% per quarter in the number of countries with transnational terrorist incidents

Figure 21. Quarterly number of countries with transnational terrorist incidents, 1993–2004.

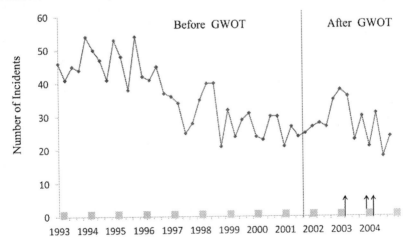

occurring within their borders over the study period ($p < .0001$). In raw numbers, this meant a decrease over the time frame of about one country per quarter with such incidents. However, the results indicated that the GWOT was associated with a significant shift in this pattern.

In this case, the onset of the War on Terrorism was associated with a 29% increase in the number of countries with transnational terrorist activity ($p = .0031$). In contrast, the capture of Saddam Hussein was associated with a significant 52% decrease ($p = .034$). In raw numbers, this meant that the onset of the GWOT added, on average, 10 more countries with activity, whereas the capture of Saddam Hussein reduced the number of countries with incidents by about 19. Although the invasion of Iraq and the release of photos from Abu Ghraib were also associated with increases (20% and 36%, respectively) in the number of countries with activity, these shifts were significant only at a trend ($p < .15$) level. This may be because these events had mixed effects, simultaneously increasing and decreasing dispersion. On the other hand, the military effort known as the GWOT appears to have had a direct stimulating effect, whereas the capture of Saddam Hussein may have demoralized would-be assailants in a number of countries. In this case, the results lend support to Hypothesis 4 but do not support Hypothesis 9.

I also hypothesized that the number and percentage of transnational terrorist incidents in countries in which more than 50% of the population could be classified as Muslim would show an increase after the start of the GWOT (Hypothesis 4b). On average, before the start of the War on Terrorism, 30% of transnational terrorist incidents each quarter were located in the 41 countries classified in the data set as having 50% or more Muslim populations.[14] However, as shown in Figure 22, the percentage of incidents in such countries climbed steadily after the onset of this event.

In the time series analysis, which was significant ($F = 12.46$; $p < .0001$), no significant effect for time was found. In other

Figure 22. Quarterly percent of transnational terrorist incidents in countries with 50% or more Muslim populations, 1993–2004.

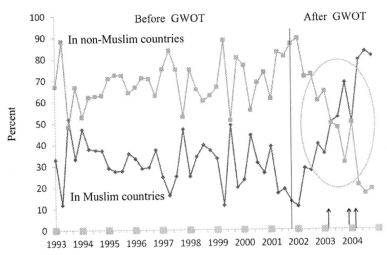

words, the percentage contribution of transnational terrorist incidents, in predominantly Muslim countries, to all incidents was not found to demonstrate any linear trend over the study period. Nor was any significant effect found for the onset of the GWOT or the capture of Saddam Hussein. However, the onset of the War in Iraq ($p < .0001$) and the release of photos from Abu Ghraib ($p = .0044$) were each associated with significant (30–32%) increases in the occurrence of incidents in Muslim countries. These results are interesting since they suggest that the onset of the War in Iraq, perceived by many Muslims as an unjust war, and the release of photos perceived by Muslims as indicative of their worst fears, stirred more antagonism (and terrorism) in Muslim countries than the GWOT, which was more widely supported in the Muslim world.

Visual inspection of the regional distribution of transnational terrorist incidents over the study period suggested a shift in the number of incidents from Europe to the Middle East and North

Africa (Figure 23). To test the extent to which the onset of the War on Terrorism was associated with a specific increase in incidents in the latter region (Hypothesis 4c), I extracted a quarterly time series representing incidents in this region as a percentage of all incidents. Visual inspection of this series (Figure 24) suggests that transnational terrorist incidents in the Middle East and North African region increased dramatically as a percentage of all incidents before the onset of the GWOT (perhaps in relation to the Palestinian Intifada in the late 1990s) but, subsequently, showed a pattern mostly of decline until mid-2004.

In the time series regression, which was statistically significant ($F = 9.14$; $p < .0001$), the onset of the War on Terrorism and the release of photos from Abu Ghraib were both found to increase incidents in the Middle East and North African region. However,

Figure 23. Quarterly number of transnational terrorist incidents by region, 1993–2004.

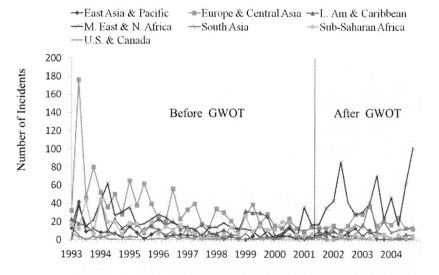

Figure 24. Quarterly percentage of transnational terrorist incidents in the Middle East and North Africa, 1993–2004.

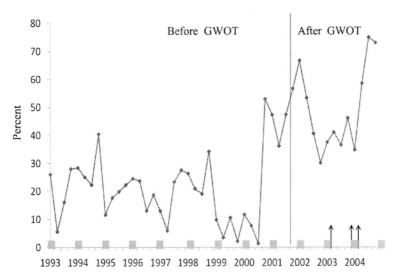

this effect was only statistically significant for the release of photos, which was associated with a 30% increase in incidents in the Middle East and North African region ($p = .028$). These results suggest that the release of photos from Abu Ghraib had a powerful effect on the frequency of terrorist activity in this part of the world.

SHIFTS IN THE TYPE OF ATTACK

Hostage Takings

My fifth hypothesis (Hypothesis 5) was that hostage takings would be found to have increased in absolute number and as a percentage of all types of attacks in association with the War on Terrorism. I also hypothesized that hostage takings would be found to have increased in association with the invasion of Iraq, the capture of Saddam Hussein, and the release of photos from Abu Ghraib (Hypothesis 9).

Figure 25. Quarterly number of bombings, assassinations, and hostage takings, 1993–2004.

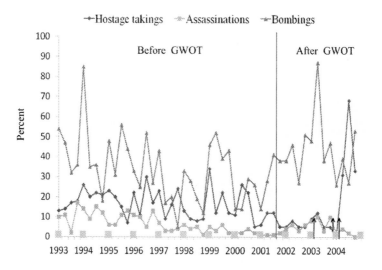

Figure 25 shows the average quarterly number of incidents for three of the most common types of attack over the period: bombings, hostage takings, and assassinations. Visual inspection of this figure suggests that hostage takings decreased, whereas bombings increased, in relation to the War on Terrorism. However, the figure also suggests that hostage takings increased in relation to the release of photos from Abu Ghraib.

The time series regression analysis confirmed these visual impressions. Contrary to my stated expectation, but consistent with previous findings of others,[15] the regression, which was statistically significant ($F = 17.4$; $p < .0001$), indicated that the onset of the War on Terrorism was associated with a significant *decline* in hostage takings ($p = .04$). (In raw numbers, there were about six fewer quarterly incidents of hostage takings after the onset of the GWOT compared with the period before, when the average number was 16.6 per quarter.) However, although the invasion of

Iraq and the capture of Saddam Hussein were not found to have any significant effect on this variable, the release of photos from Abu Ghraib was associated with a significant increase ($p < .0001$) in this type of attack. (In raw numbers, there were about 50 more quarterly incidents of hostage takings after Abu Ghraib.)[16]

I found similar results when I examined the percentage contribution of hostage takings to all types of attack. According to this analysis, which was also significant ($F = 11.9; p < .0001$), the War on Terrorism was associated with a 23% decrease in hostage takings ($p < .0001$), whereas Abu Ghraib was associated with a 29% increase in this type of attack ($p = .011$).

Bombings
Since Enders and Sandler found that bombings as a percentage of all transnational terrorist incidents increased (although hostage takings decreased) after the start of the War on Terrorism, I also examined the effects of the GWOT and the other predictor events on this variable. In this case, the time series, which was significant ($F = 5.38; p = .0007$), showed that bombings, as a percentage of all incidents, decreased by about half of one percentage point over the study period ($p = .0022$). I did not find any significant effect on this variable for the start of the GWOT or the invasion of Iraq. However, I did find a significant association between bombings as a percentage of all incidents and the release of photos from Abu Ghraib ($p = .011$). In this case, the release of photos was associated with a 26% *decrease* in bombings as a percentage of all types of incidents. This effect on the percentage share of bombings is likely to have been a function of the large increase in hostage takings associated with Abu Ghraib.

Assassinations
I also examined the effects of the GWOT and the other predictor variables on the percentage of incidents classified as assassinations.

This analysis, which was significant ($F = 2.86$; $p = .01$), indicated a trend for assassinations to decrease by 3.1 percentage points ($p = .0032$) over the time period. However, I did not detect any significant changes in this pattern associated with the predictor variables (the onset of the GWOT, the start of the War in Iraq, capture of Saddam Hussein, or the release of photos from Abu Ghraib).

Shifts in the Type of Victim

My sixth hypothesis was that the War on Terrorism would be shown to have led to an increase in incidents in which the victim(s) were multinational (i.e., an international organization or victims were from more than one country) (Hypothesis 6). I also hypothesized that incidents with multinational victims would be found to have increased in association with the invasion of Iraq, the capture of Saddam Hussein, and the release of photos from Abu Ghraib (Hypothesis 9).

The mean number of quarterly incidents with multinational victims in the preintervention period was 32 ± 15.4. Visual inspection of the time series for the number of attacks with multinational victims (Figure 26) suggests a clear linear trend of incidents with multinational victims decreasing before the War on Terrorism and increasing afterwards. The time series analysis, which was significant ($F = 7.42$; $p = .0007$), confirmed a trend of a 3% decline ($p < .0001$) in the number of incidents with multinational victims over the study period.

However, in support of Hypothesis 6 and in partial support of Hypothesis 9, the onset of the War on Terrorism and the other events were clearly associated with shifts in this pattern. Specifically, the results of the regression indicated that when the other events were held constant, the release of photos from Abu Ghraib was associated with a significant 141% increase in incidents with

Figure 26. Quarterly number of transnational terrorist incidents with a multinational victim, 1993–2004.

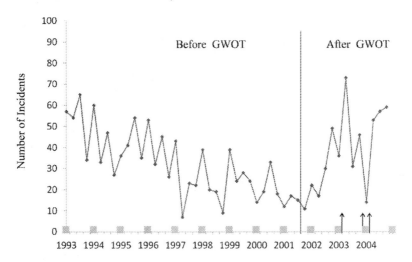

multinational victims (p = .008). Moreover, the GWOT was associated with a closer to significant (p ≤ .06) 53% increase in such incidents, whereas the war in Iraq was associated with a similarly closer to significant (p < .06) 72% increase and the capture of Saddam Hussein was associated with a 103% decrease (p < .06).

These results are likely to be related to the increasing availability of multinational civilian targets engaged in reconstruction on the ground after the onset of the war in Afghanistan and the start of the war in Iraq. However, they are disturbing since a stated purpose of the War on Terrorism and the subsequent invasion of Iraq was to protect the citizens of the world's nations, not just those of the United States.

On the other hand, inspection of the percentage distribution of incidents with multinational victims as a percentage of all incidents suggests a somewhat different story. As shown in Figure 27, the

Figure 27. Quarterly percent of transnational terrorist incidents with a multinational victim, 1993–2004.

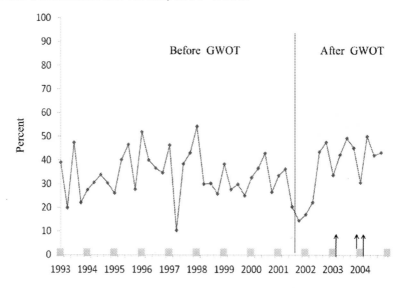

contribution of incidents with multinational victims as a percentage of all incidents showed very little change over the total study period. This figure suggests that changes in the percentage of transnational terrorist incidents with multinational victims may simply reflect changes in the total numbers of incidents.

My seventh hypothesis was that the War on Terrorism would be found to be associated with a *decline* in transnational terrorist incidents in which one or more victims were U.S. citizens (Hypothesis 7). I also hypothesized that the number of incidents with at least one U.S. victim would be found to have increased in association with the invasion of Iraq, the capture of Saddam Hussein, and the release of photos from Abu Ghraib (Hypothesis 9).

My results, however, failed to confirm either of the proposed hypotheses. In fact, in this case, the time series regression itself was not significant ($F = 1.3$; $p = .267$). This may be because this

Figure 28. Quarterly number of transnational terrorist incidents with one or more U.S. victims, 1993–2004 (persons or property).

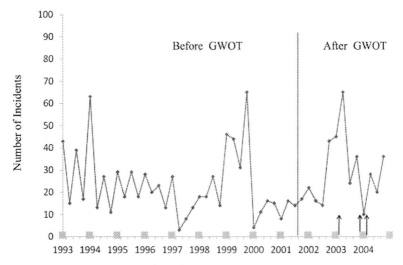

variable showed so much fluctuation before the onset of the War on Terrorism (Figure 28) that it was not possible to capture any lasting effect in the postintervention period.

Nor did visual inspection of the percentage distribution of transnational terrorist incidents with U.S. victims indicate much change at all in association with the War on Terrorism or the other events of interest (the invasion of Iraq, the capture of Saddam Hussein, and the release of photos from Abu Ghraib). As shown in Figure 29, the incidents with U.S. victims, as a percentage of all incidents, showed relatively little fluctuation after the onset of the War on Terrorism.

Attacks Against People or Property
I did not apply time series to analyze change in incidents involving people as opposed to property. Visual evidence, however, does suggest that attacks against people, as opposed to property, increased dramatically after the Abu Ghraib incident (Figure 30).

Figure 29. Quarterly percent of transnational terrorist incidents with one or more U.S. victims, 1993–2004.

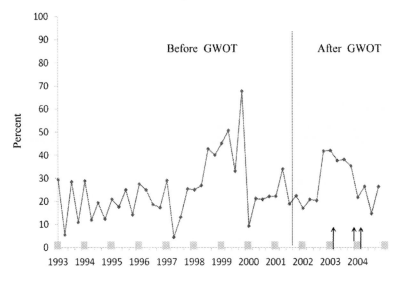

Figure 30. Quarterly number of transnational terrorist incidents against people, property, or both targets, 1993–2004.

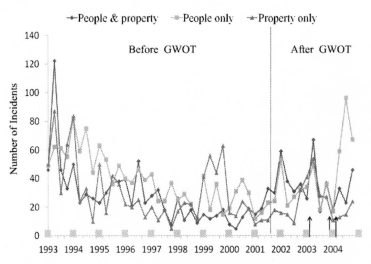

Shifts in "Islamist" Perpetrated Terrorism

My next hypothesis was that the War on Terrorism would be shown to have escalated so-called Islamist transnational terrorism; that is, transnational terrorist incidents perpetrated by known Islamist or Islamist national separatist groups (Hypothesis 8). I also hypothesized that the other predictor events would have escalating effects on "Islamist" transnational terrorism.

The average quarterly number of incidents that could be attributed in the data set to known "Islamist" terrorist organizations before the War on Terrorism was 12.1 ± 7.7 (range 1–32 incidents). Visual inspection of the time series (Figure 31) shows a pattern of decline from the early mid-1990s through the year 2000, a small increase in late 2001, a spike in mid-2003, and a more gradual but steady climb in incidents in the second quarter in mid-2004.

The time series regression, which was statistically significant ($F = 6.99$; $p = .00002$), did not detect any significant effect for time

Figure 31. Quarterly number of transnational terrorist incidents attributed to "Islamist" terrorist organizations, 1993–2004.

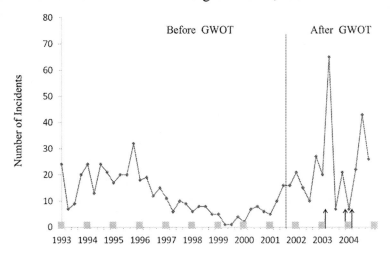

over the study period. However, it did show that the onset of the
War on Terrorism, the invasion of Iraq, and the release of photos
from Abu Ghraib were all associated with upward shifts in the
number of such transnational terrorist incidents, whereas the capture
of Saddam Hussein was associated with a downward shift. Of these
shifts, the largest contribution, increasing such incidents by 135%,
came from the release of photos from Abu Ghraib and this event
was the only one that was statistically significant ($p = .049$).

These results suggest, once again, that the evidence of abuse
at Abu Ghraib had a powerful effect. As noted earlier, 50% of all
attacks in the data set could not be attributed to a known terrorist
group, and unclaimed attacks (without "calling cards") have been
a hallmark of al Qaeda and its affiliates and related terrorist organizations for some time.[17] The dramatic and significant increase in
attacks that were claimed by or could be *attributed* to such groups
after Abu Ghraib suggests that this event had a persistent emboldening effect. Although the onset of the GWOT and the invasion of
Iraq were each also associated with upwards shifts in such claimed
or "attributable" incidents, the effects were more short lived, pos-
sibly because the perpetrators subsequently melted into the shadows or stopped leaving "calling cards."

I also hypothesized that incidents that could be attributed to
"Islamist" terrorist groups, as a percentage of all incidents, would
escalate in relation to the GWOT and the other predictor events of
interest. This expectation was not confirmed. Although the time series
regression showed that the GWOT, as well as the invasion of Iraq and
the release of photos, were all associated with escalation (Figure 32),
none of the effects were statistically significant. This should not be
taken to mean that incidents perpetrated by such groups did not escalate. It is more likely that the percentage of incidents that could be
attributed simply fluctuated as such groups came in and out of the
shadows, at times claiming attacks and at times not doing so.

Figure 32. Quarterly percent of transnational terrorist incidents attributed to "Islamist" terrorist organizations, 1993–2004.

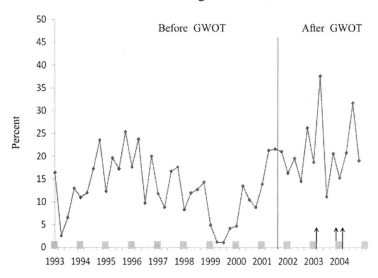

SUMMARY OF FINDINGS

In summary, the time series analyses of the merged data suggest that the onset of the War on Terrorism was significantly associated ($p < .05$) with a downward shift in the percentage of all incidents that were hostage takings but with increases in the *frequency* of transnational terrorist incidents (number of incidents, number of days with incidents), *dispersion* (number of countries with incidents), *lethality* (number of deadly incidents), and at the $p < .06$ level in the number of incidents with *multinational victims*. Of these, the magnitude of increase was greatest for the number of deadly incidents.

In contrast, the invasion of Iraq was found to be associated only with significant increases ($p < .05$) in the percentage share of incidents in Muslim countries and at the trend level ($p < .06$) in the number of incidents with multinational victims.

Contrary to expectation, the capture of Saddam Hussein was actually associated with significant decreases ($p < .05$) on three of the outcome measures: the number of incidents, the number of days with transnational terrorist activity, and the number of countries with such activity.

Conversely, the release of photos from Abu Ghraib was significantly associated with an escalation on most of the outcome measures: number of incidents, number of days of incidents, incidents in Muslim countries and incidents in the Middle East as percentages of all incidents, hostage takings as a percentage of all types of attacks, number of incidents with multinational victims, number of incidents by known "Islamist" terrorist groups, and at the trend level ($p < .06$), number of lethal incidents (Figure 33 and Table 1). These results, because they are statistically

Figure 33. Summary graph of ARIMA results, all incidents.

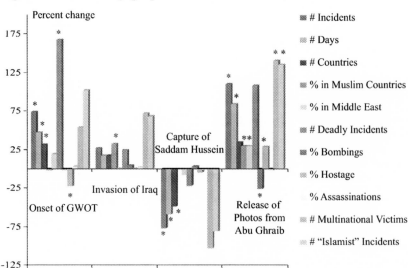

Table 1. Summary table of time series (ARIMA) results.

Outcome	Intervention	Coefficient	t-Stat.	Prob.		Percentage change
No. of incidents						
	GWOT	0.735	4.534	0.0001	*	+74
	Invasion of Iraq	0.266	1.241	0.2222		
	Capture Hussein	-0.774	-2.030	0.049	*	-77
	Abu Ghraib	1.097	2.99	0.0048	*	+109
No. of days						
	GWOT	0.467	5.185	0.0001	*	+47
	Invasion of Iraq	-0.0167	1.270	0.2119		
	Capture Hussein	-0.582	-2.350	0.024	*	-59
	Abu Ghraib	0.843	3.538	0.0011	*	+84
No. of deadly incidents						
	GWOT	1.676	7.836	0.0001	*	+168
	Invasion of Iraq	0.239	0.870	0.3899		
	Capture Hussein	-0.224	-0.403	0.6887		
	Abu Ghraib	1.086	1.919	0.063	<	+108
Percentage of deadly incidents						
	GWOT	0.162	3.314	0.002	*	+16
	Invasion of Iraq	0.009	0.154	0.879		
	Capture Hussein	0.111	1.079	0.288		
	Abu Ghraib	0.0726	0.719	0.477		

(continued)

Table 1. (continued) Summary table of time series (ARIMA) results.

Outcome	Intervention	Coefficient	t-Stat.	Prob.		Percentage change
No. of countries						
	GWOT	0.288	3.162	0.003	*	+29
	Invasion of Iraq	0.205	1.572	0.124		
	Capture Hussein	-0.521	-2.199	0.034	*	-52
	Abu Ghraib	0.357	1.530	0.13		
Percentage in Muslim countries						
	GWOT	-0.018	-0.360	0.720		
	Invasion of Iraq	0.330	5.251	0.0001	*	+33
	Capture Hussein	-0.045	-0.446	0.659		
	Abu Ghraib	0.295	3.040	0.0044	*	+30
Percentage in Middle East and North Africa						
	GWOT	0.191	1.690	0.099		
	Invasion of Iraq	0.007	0.058	0.954		
	Capture Hussein	-0.077	-0.598	0.553		
	Abu Ghraib	0.296	2.228	0.028	*	+30
Percentage of hostage takings						
	GWOT	-0.23	-5.67	0.0001	*	-23
	Invasion of Iraq	0.006	0.096	0.924		
	Capture Hussein	-0.0498	-0.463	0.646		
	Abu Ghraib	0.289	2.672	0.0111	*	+29

(continued)

Outcome	Intervention	Coefficient	t-Stat.	Prob.		Percentage change
Percentage of bombings						
	GWOT	-0.0157	-0.281	0.780		
	Invasion of Iraq	0.045	0.660	0.5129		
	Capture Hussein	0.030	0.260	0.796		
	Abu Ghraib	-0.26	-2.242	0.031	*	-26
Percentage of assassinations						
	GWOT	0.027	1.37	0.179		
	Invasion of Iraq	0.022	0.932	0.357		
	Capture Hussein	-0.016	-0.450	0.655		
	Abu Ghraib	-0.024	-0.66	0.511		
No. of incidents with multinational victims						
	GWOT	0.535	1.984	0.0545	<	+54
	Invasion of Iraq	0.719	2.022	0.0502	<	+72
	Capture Hussein	-1.031	-1.996	0.0532	<	-103
	Abu Ghraib	1.408	2.825	0.008	*	+140
No. of incidents with U.S. victims						
	GWOT	0.483	1.17	0.249		
	Invasion of Iraq	0.398	0.728	0.4713		
	Capture Hussein	-0.893	-1.232	0.226		
	Abu Ghraib	0.697	0.9723	0.337		

(continued)

Table 1. *(continued)* Summary table of time series (ARIMA) results.

Outcome	Intervention	Coefficient	*t*-Stat.	Prob.	Percentage change
No. of "Islamist" incidents					
	GWOT	1.027	1.676	0.1019	
	Invasion of Iraq	0.681	1.177	0.246	
	Capture Hussein	−0.806	−1.129	0.266	
	Abu Ghraib	1.353	2.02	0.0499 *	+135
Percentage of "Islamist" incidents					
	GWOT	4.017	0.69	0.494	
	Invasion of Iraq	5.06	0.919	0.3636	
	Capture Hussein	−4.151	−0.571	0.5711	
	Abu Ghraib	8.475	1.239	0.222	

* p < 0.05, ^ p < 0.06

significant and also converge, suggest that Abu Ghraib had a powerful effect on subsequent terrorism.[18]

When events in Israel and the Occupied Territories were excluded from the analysis of number of incidents and number of deadly incidents, somewhat different results were obtained. As shown in Figure 34 and Table 2, the onset of the War on Terrorism was not found to have significantly increased the number of incidents although it was still found to have increased the number of deadly incidents. On the other hand, the invasion of Iraq and the release of photos from Abu Ghraib were both found to have significant statistical effects on the number of incidents and the number of deadly incidents. These results suggest that the invasion of Iraq, in addition to Abu Ghraib, was key to subsequent transnational terrorism outside Israel and the Occupied Territories.[19]

Figure 34. Summary graph of ARIMA results, Israel and Occupied Territories excluded.

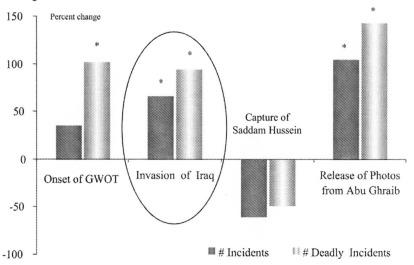

Table 2. Summary table of time series (ARIMA) results, Israel and Occupied Territories excluded.

Outcome	Intervention	Coefficient	t-Stat.	Prob.		Percentage change
No. of incidents (Israel excluded)						
	GWOT	0.35	1.59	0.12		
	Invasion of Iraq	0.657	2.163	0.037	*	+65
	Capture Hussein	−0.601	−1.464	0.151		
	Abu Ghraib	1.04	2.70	0.014	*	+104
No. of deadly incidents (Israel excluded)						
	GWOT	1.021	4.510	0.0001	*	+102
	Invasion of Iraq	0.94	3.018	0.0045	*	+94
	Capture Hussein	−0.484	−0.833	0.410		
	Abu Ghraib	1.428	2.488	0.0174	*	+143

* $p < 0.05$, ^ $p < 0.06$

CHAPTER 7

CONCLUSIONS

What is of supreme importance in war is to attack the enemy's strategy.

Therefore I say: "know the enemy and know yourself; in a hundred battles you will never be in peril."

—Sun Tzu

As they say, "If you would seek war, prepare for war."

I believe, my lord, the saying is "If you would seek peace, prepare for war," Leonard ventured.
Vetinari put his head on one side and his lips moved as he repeated the phrase to himself. Finally he said, "No, no, I just don't see that one at all."

—Terry Pratchett, Jingo

This research began with a question: "Has the Global War on Terrorism, with its underlying strategy of preemptive force, decreased transnational terrorist activity, or has it had the reverse effect and widened this threat?" I also wanted to find out to what extent associated events, including the invasion of Iraq, the capture of Iraq's former dictator, Saddam Hussein, and evidence after Abu Ghraib of U.S. soldiers abusing Iraqi detainees, might have affected this dynamic.

Based on strategic interaction and resource mobilization theory, as well as conflict escalation theory and previous research relating to domestic terrorism, I expected that the data in this study would show that the military effort known as the GWOT and the other events would have an escalatory effect on transnational terrorist activity. The results supported these expectations with some exceptions.

Consistent with the force escalation hypothesis, the onset of the War on Terrorism was found to be associated with a statistical increase in the quarterly frequency, dispersion, and lethality of subsequent transnational terrorist activity. The release of photos of prisoner abuse from Abu Ghraib was also found to be associated with increases in the quarterly frequency and lethality of subsequent transnational terrorism. Surprisingly, the invasion of Iraq was not associated with upward shifts in the frequency or lethality of transnational terrorist incidents. This may be because the onset of the war in Iraq occurred at a time when terrorist incidents in Israel and the Occupied Territories (which spiked after the onset of the GWOT) were on a decline. A separate analysis (with Israel and the Occupied Territories excluded for the full time series) indicated that the invasion of Iraq was significantly associated with a shift toward more transnational terrorist incidents and more deadly ones. Although I expected that the capture of Iraq's dictator, Saddam Hussein, would have an escalating effect, this was not the case. Indeed, the opposite appeared to happen.

I also hypothesized that the War on Terrorism and the related events would be associated with a shift in the tactics of those engaging in transnational terrorism. Specifically, I expected that hostage taking would be shown to increase in absolute number and as a percentage of all types of attacks in relation to the War on Terrorism and the other events. I found only partial support for this hypothesis. In fact, the data showed that hostage takings decreased after the onset of the War on Terrorism. Conversely, the release of photos of abuse from Abu Ghraib was associated with a steep increase in the absolute number and percentage of hostage takings. In addition, I expected that the War on Terrorism and the other events would lead to an upward shift in the number of incidents with multinational victims and a downward shift in the number of incidents with U.S. victims. The former hypothesis was supported for the onset of the War on Terrorism and the invasion of Iraq. Moreover, the evidence suggested an upward trend for Abu Ghraib. However, there was no evidence from the data to show that the number of incidents with U.S. victims changed after the onset of the War on Terrorism or any of the other events. Finally, I hypothesized that incidents known to be perpetrated by Islamist terrorist organizations would increase in relation to each of the predictor variables. This expectation was confirmed only for the effect of the release of photos of prisoner abuse from Abu Ghraib.

Clearly, the results presented here need to be treated with caution for all the methodological reasons outlined at the end of chapter 5. Most important, the caveat needs to be repeated that although cause and effect can be inferred, they cannot be conclusively demonstrated in time series intervention analyses.[1] Such designs, because they are not experimental, cannot control for the counterfactual (what might have happened if no policy of preemptive force had been declared and no War on Terrorism had occurred). Nor can such designs prove that an apparently key or critical event was necessarily *the* key or critical event in the shift in a series of observations. It is always possible that other factors, over and above those studied, were more important. For example, in relation to the results of this study, the argument could be made that the critical variable for mobilization was not the War on Terrorism and that the real catalyst was 9/11 itself. The argument could also be made that it is too early to measure the impact of the GWOT, and a case could be made that different sources or measures (e.g., number of casualties instead of number of incidents with casualties) or different units of analysis (e.g., days or years rather than quarters) or methods might produce different results.

Still, the findings of this study are compelling. How do they fit with existing theory? What avenues for further research do they suggest? And what policy lessons can be learned from them?

IMPLICATIONS FOR THEORY

In relation to theory, several observations can be made. First, the evidence suggests that the employment of force as a response to transnational terrorism does escalate the frequency and lethality of such activity. The clear trend of decreasing events in the 1990s was significantly shifted after the onset of the War on Terrorism and the invasion of Afghanistan. These results lend support to resource mobilization models of terrorism, and they also extend conflict escalation theories to transnational terrorism. In addition, the results call into question the wisdom of policies that place a heavy reliance on "hard tactics" as a means of combating or preempting transnational terrorism. In fact, the results suggest that such tactics may be counterproductive.

Second, the evidence suggests that these effects are magnified when force disintegrates into "barbarism," as it did at Abu Ghraib. These results lend support to and extend Ivan Arreguin-Toft's theoretical construct of the negative effects of barbarism and violation of the laws of war in asymmetric conflicts. The release of photographs of U.S. soldiers abusing Iraqis was not, as Fareed Zakaria has put it, just "bad public relations":

> Ask any soldier in Iraq when the general population really turned against the United States and he will say, "Abu Ghraib." A few months before the scandal broke, Coalition Provisional Authority polls showed Iraqi support for the occupation at 63 percent. A month after Abu Ghraib, the number was 9 percent. Polls showed that 71 percent of Iraqis were surprised by the revelations. Most telling, 61 percent of Iraqis polled believed that no one would be punished for the torture at Abu Ghraib. Of the 29 percent who said they believed someone would be punished, 52 percent said that such punishment would extend only to "the little people."[2]

One lesson from the results presented here might be that if you brutalize the enemy there will be negative consequences.

Third, the evidence suggests that transnational terrorism may become more dispersed when larger numbers of countries join a military counterterrorism effort (as happened after the invasion of Afghanistan) and less dispersed when the coalition effort is smaller (as it was at the time of the invasion of Iraq). These results lend support to rational choice models in which terrorists maximize utility by adapting their efforts and tactics to achieve desired effects. Although the change in dispersion may simply have been coincidental, it is likely that a tactic of more attacks in more countries was specifically designed by the leaders of some terrorist groups to deter governments from participating in further coalition efforts. Conversely, a tactic of concentrating attacks in a few countries, especially Muslim countries, after the invasion of Iraq, was undoubtedly designed to punish those governments that supported or turned a blind eye to that military effort. The change in dispersion has implications for collective action models of transnational terrorism. As Bueno de Mesquita observes, governments confronted with transnational terrorism face choices. They can choose to act in concert or they can "free ride." One implication of the results found here is the possibility that when governments free ride, they may buy protection within their borders.[3] Conversely, when they participate or lend support to a military coalition, they may take the brunt of the consequences. This was certainly true for countries such as Spain and Turkey and later Britain after the invasion of Iraq.

Fourth, as a caveat to Observation 3, the free ride may not be as free as it appears. Although dispersion decreased in association with the more limited coalition in Iraq, the number of incidents with multinational victims was significantly increased. One implication of these results, which may be a function of the greater availability of multinational targets on the Afghan and Iraqi battlefields, is that a multinational military effort, no matter how large or small the coalition, may still make multinational groups of individuals and multinational organizations such as the UN and Red Cross more vulnerable.

Fifth, the evidence suggests that capturing or neutralizing a significant enemy leader is likely to have a deterrent effect at least in the short term. Almost all the measures of transnational terrorist activity studied here showed a downward turn after the capture of Saddam Hussein. Once again, these results may have been coincidental. However, it is also likely that the capture of Iraq's former leader had a demoralizing effect and made it more difficult for terrorist recruitment.

Sixth, different interventions on the part of governments appear to provoke different responses from terrorists in terms of the type of attack. In a previous study, Enders and Sandler found that the onset of the War on Terrorism, beginning with the invasion of Afghanistan, was associated with a decline in "logistically complex" types of attacks such as hostage takings.[4] They theorized that such attacks, which are costly in terms of time and resources to mount, were disrupted by the War on Terrorism. They further theorized that *less* logistically complex attacks (bombings and armed attacks) were "substituted." My results, using a larger data set, confirm these findings. As such they lend support to the rational choice theory of terrorism and the concept of "substitution" effects.

However, according to the evidence presented here, the release of photos of prisoner abuse from Abu Ghraib changed this trend. After Abu Ghraib, hostage takings went up. Moreover, barbaric methods of treating hostages (beheadings) increased. These effects suggest that terrorists may calculate the utility of certain tactics on the basis of considerations such as symbolism and not just direct costs. In addition, and in support of resource mobilization models, it may be argued that Abu Ghraib was good (symbolically) for terrorist recruitment and hence made such "logistically complex" attacks more feasible.

Seventh, none of the interventions produced evidence of an upward or downward shift in the number of transnational terrorist incidents with U.S. victims. These findings, suggesting that the vulnerability of U.S. noncombatant targets remained the same, have major implications for policy. As has been repeatedly pointed out by members of the Bush administration, it is true that no catastrophic incident such as 9/11 has occurred on U.S. soil since the onset of the War on Terrorism. Nonetheless, given the cost of the effort in U.S. treasure and soldiers' lives lost, one might have expected to see a decline.

Finally, the evidence suggests that Abu Ghraib, more than any of the other events, was associated with significant increases in incidents by Islamist extremist terrorist organizations. These results, suggesting an emboldening effect, lend further weight to strategic interaction and resource mobilization models of terrorism. In addition, they highlight the important lesson that hard tactics plus barbarism do not have the desired effect of curbing terrorist activity and, in fact, the reverse is often true.

IMPLICATIONS FOR RESEARCH

To Senator Feingold's question, "How do we measure this thing?", I have tried to provide an answer using a time series intervention analysis of existing data from two sources. Other avenues of research that could build on and extend these findings include the following:

First, there is a need for better constructs and better taxonomies of terrorism and counterterrorism.[5] Qualitative methods, such as content analysis, and also frame and discourse analysis, could be used to refine and extend our understanding of these constructs.

Second, there is a need for more comprehensive data. Current terrorism data sets are limited for the most part to transnational terrorism.[6] Domestic terrorist acts, however, often have implications for transnational terrorism but cannot be captured using existing data. Other sources, for example, police archives, could provide enriched datasets.[7] Case studies, using multiple methods (e.g., survey, intensive interviews, participant observation) and multiple informants, could also shed new light on the research questions addressed here.

A third need is for studies based on other time spans and other units of analysis. The current project should be expanded to include more recent data. It is possible that the U.S.–Iraqi offensive in Fallujah in November 2004 had a further escalating effect (or conversely, a deescalating effect) since as many as 1,200 insurgents were killed in that offensive.[8] The use of more refined units of analysis (e.g., monthly data) could also enrich and potentially cast new light on the findings presented in this study. It may also be fruitful to examine "campaigns" of transnational terrorism and conduct more fine-grained analyses of specific types of terrorist acts.[9]

Fourth, the value of coding and analyzing terrorist acts and counterterrorist responses in sequences should be considered. Such analyses could capture more immediate effects of counterterrorism. They could also shed light on a question not addressed here. That is, "How do terrorist acts affect counterterrorist responses?"[10]

Finally, different methods should be used as alternatives or adjuncts to the approach used here.[11] One of the limitations of using aggregate events data is that such data cannot be used to evaluate the impact of policies or strategies on individuals, and how those policies change motivations, preferences, or even individual behavior. We do not know, for example, how the articulated policy of preemptive force, or its implementation on the ground, have altered the motivations, preferences, and behavior of individual participants in terrorist activities or those who, in the normal course of events, might stand on the sidelines. Such evaluations require intensive case study methods.[12] Nor do we know the extent to which policies, such as the one studied here, have different impacts across space (countries, cultures) and time. To address this gap and enhance our understanding of the comparative impact of such policies, focused case comparison studies could be conducted.[13] There is also a need for research that better incorporates the "counterfactual" (what might have happened in the absence of the policy studied here and its implementation). Although historical problems, such as the one addressed here, are not amenable to experimental manipulation, logical chains of causality can be enhanced by using methods such as process tracing,[14] experimental simulation,[15] and intensive studies of cases over time.

IMPLICATIONS FOR POLICY

Given the findings presented here, "What can be done?" The history of domestic terrorism indicates that terrorist groups often burn out when they lose outside support.[16] However, history also shows that the use of coercive force by governments can have a stimulating effect and that force, especially when perceived as illegitimate, can radicalize moderates. In particular, it can "undermine restraints against the use of violence both nationally and internationally" and contribute to a "tit-for-tat upward spiral in the level and indiscriminateness of violence."[17] In addition, the use of force, when perceived as illegitimate or unjust, can lead to what Ehud Sprinzak calls a "crisis of legitimacy" in which ordinary people become so enraged that they begin to accept the logic of terrorism as a response to violence on the part of governments.[18]

If a heavy reliance on military force as a means of preempting transnational terrorism is not the most effective policy choice, what course should the United States take? The results presented here do not provide a blueprint for policy. A logical inference, however, is that terrorist financing and recruitment need to be curtailed. One way to reduce terrorist financing and recruitment would be to focus more resources on the sources of terrorist support and sympathy.

A basic assumption behind this book is that terrorism is politically motivated and calculated. Among other goals, bin Laden, in particular, has repeatedly stressed his goal of driving foreign troops from the Arabian Peninsula and Muslim holy lands.[19] Pew polls suggest that this goal has resonance in the Arab and Muslim world. To the degree that the United States keeps troops in Iraq and the Arabian Peninsula, bin Laden and his followers are likely to continue to receive support and gain recruits. *One policy implication of this study is that the United States needs to develop a plan to withdraw militarily from Iraq and the Arabian Peninsula.*

Bin Laden and his group and offshoots are also committed to mobilizing the Muslim world for what might be called "the Muslim Nation"—by projecting the confrontation with the United States and its coalition as a battle of "Islam against infidelity,"[20] or in Huntington's words, "a clash of civilizations."[21] The results presented here suggest that terrorist mobilization and support were enhanced, especially in the Middle East and in Muslim nations, after the release of photos of U.S. soldiers abusing and humiliating detainees at Abu Ghraib. *Another policy implication is that the United States has to take a higher ground and renounce abuse and torture. Whatever its merits in terms of intelligence, its overall effect is counterproductive.*

Given al Qaeda's goal of building a Muslim nation by projecting an "us against them" mentality, the United States should also be careful about how it articulates its war on terrorism. *In particular, it needs to avoid calling it a "civilization war" as the president did in a speech in October 2005.*[22] Such characterizations are likely to have an inflaming effect.

Tactically, al Qaeda and its offshoots have mobilized support by focusing attention on conflicts the international community has previously avoided; for example, conflicts in Kashmir and Chechnya. *To decrease support for al Qaeda and its offshoots and imitators, the United States and the international community may need to pay closer attention to the solution of such conflicts.*

Al Qaeda and other such groups have also gained stature and legitimacy in parts of the Muslim world by doing "good works" and by associating themselves with Islamist movements that fill vacuums their countries have neglected.[23] Such groups are known to provide charity in their community. In addition, they provide an infrastructure for dissent against repressive governments. Today, Islamist political movements are gaining ground in many countries and are fast becoming, in the words of the editor of Dubai's *Khaleej Times*, "the key political players in the Middle East."[24] This is not a trend the United States can afford to ignore. As visiting Carnegie Endowment Fellow, Mustapha Kamel Al-Sayyid observes, "many Muslims blame the West for the suffering inflicted by their dictators," and Pew polls show that increasing numbers sympathize with the causes if not the tactics of extremist Islamist terrorist groups. To the extent that the United States continues to lump all Islamist groups together and does not distinguish between those committed to a pluralistic political process and those committed to violence, it will only increase resentment and "play into the hands of those who use terrorism to further their objectives at home and against the west."[25] *Another policy implication of the results found here may be that the United States needs to engage moderate Islamists and stop partnering with governments that abuse human rights.*

As a tactic, Joseph Nye has argued that the employment of "hard power," designed to coerce and preempt, needs to be complemented by "soft power," based on the ability to persuade and "shape the preferences of others."[26] Soft power in the form of public diplomacy was once one of the hallmarks of U.S. foreign policy. The use of soft power, however, has declined in recent years. In fact, Nye argues that the United States currently spends as much as 450 times more on hard power as on soft power. One result has been that international polls have shown dramatic declines in the popularity of the United States (see *Pew Global Attitudes Surveys* available at http://people-press.org) around the world. These declines were particularly sharp after the invasion of Iraq.[27]

This does not mean that the United States needs to abandon hard power altogether. Rather, a balance of hard and soft power may be required. Against a resolute adversary such as al Qaeda, the United States must continue to use its military, intelligence, and police forces to secure potential targets and defend its citizens and installations at home and abroad. However, it must do so with the understanding that 100% security is impossible since individuals bent on transnational terrorism only need to be successful once. In Brian Jenkins' words, they "can attack anything, anywhere, anytime, whereas it is not possible to protect everything, everywhere, all the time."[28]

Against an enemy such as al Qaeda, force may also be necessary for some time. Eliminating al Qaeda leaders bent on killing U.S. citizens and others has to remain a priority. For this mission, the United States must continue to develop its military capacity to wage small counterinsurgency campaigns to destroy terrorist resources and capture their leaders without resorting to barbarism. Flexible, fast, and discriminate forces remain essential for specific missions as Posen recommends.[29]

In this contest, the U.S. will also require a broad-based globalized strategy that in Cronin's words "seamlessly" incorporates "international economic, political, legal, diplomatic, cultural and military elements."[30]

At the same time, the U.S. government may need to recognize that the power of those engaging in transnational terrorism and specifically "Islamist" jihadi terrorism is a function of the extent to which these individuals and groups capture hearts and minds and the United States fails to do so. To the extent that the United States continues to partner with governments that repress their people and abuse human rights, it is unlikely to win hearts and minds in the Muslim world.

To win hearts and minds, the United States needs to engage moderate Islamists. One means of achieving this objective through soft power might be to use incentives or rewards. Unfortunately, the concept of using incentives has not received wide attention in policy circles where the dominant view has been that of Machiavelli: "It is safer to be feared than loved."[31] Offering rewards, however, can be an important way of exerting influence as Martin Patchen and others have observed.[32]

David Cortright, in a review of the concept, points out that inducements in statecraft may be unconditional, designed to make cooperation more feasible, or graduated and conditioned on particular actions or responses by a recipient.[33] In November 2005 former President Bill Clinton pointed out that although the war in Iraq did not "win us friends in the Muslim world, when we rushed into Indonesia to help after the Tsunami, the favorable impression of the U.S. soared from 35% to 65% and the popularity of Osama bin Laden plummeted from 58% to 28%."[34] This observation confirms the powerful effect of unconditional efforts such as the Tsunami relief effort. Other unconditional efforts, such as building hospitals for children, are likely to bring about a similar response.

Conditional inducements and conciliatory moves, however, may also be helpful. Although the current administration has not wanted to appear in any way to be involved in appeasing the enemy, backdoor channels have been successful in working out agreements with terrorist groups in the past. For example, it is now well known that secret talks between Sinn Fein, the political arm of the Irish Republican Army, and the British government (up to and including John Major) led to a ceasefire in 1994 and were a prelude to the all-party peace process that ensued. Opening channels of communication with Islamist political groups could lead to a better understanding of what issues are most important to these groups and what gestures might be made to secure their assistance to restrain militant extremists.

In general, *graduated, reciprocated initiatives in tension reduction* have been found to be the most effective ones. This strategy, which Charles Osgood labeled GRIT, involves employing a series of conciliatory measures to reduce tensions and distrust. According to Cortright, the Bush–Gorbachev nuclear reductions at the end of the Cold War followed the GRIT strategy and "helped to dispel the decades-long clouds of fear and distrust that obstructed East-West understanding."[35] Such moves can lead to "turning points" in negotiations between adversary groups.[36]

Previous research suggests that incentives work best when they focus on limited, single objectives and are sustained over time. These considerations suggest that broad promises (such as the promise of bringing democracy to the Middle East, waging war to "save civilization itself," or relieving poverty in the Muslim world) are unlikely to be as successful as more focused ones. To win the support of moderate Islamists, a first step might be to make a limited offer to help them achieve political recognition in countries, such as Egypt, where their parties are currently banned. Such a move might be tied to cooperation in promoting nonviolent solutions and working to restrain supporters who might otherwise participate in violence.[37]

Although such strategies might be anathema to those who are on a mission to create democracies in a Western image in the Middle East and elsewhere, a key lesson from Vietnam, as former defense secretary Robert McNamara observed, is the error of thinking "We're on a mission... . We don't have the God-given right to shape every nation to our own image."[38] When, shortly after September 11, U.S. President George W. Bush declared at the U.S. National Cathedral that our "responsibility to history is...to rid the world of evil," many individual Muslims took offense.[39] As Atran observes, pitting the United States' moral world of good against the jihadist world of evil directly parallels the jihadist division of the world between "The House of Islam" (*Dar al-Islam*) and "The House of War" (*Dar al-Harb*) and feeds jihadism's religious conviction and zeal, as well as its power to persuade recruits.[40]

Barry Posen points out that the United States may have been "spoiled" because of its Cold War and Gulf War successes in attracting allies.[41] The situation today is very different. With a few possible exceptions, international terrorism is not encouraged or supported by the governments of Muslim countries. However, it is encouraged and supported by many activists who would like to see these repressive governments toppled and replaced.[42]

If the United States wants to undo the damage it has done through an excess of reliance on hard power, it needs to reach out to and listen to needs and concerns within moderate Islamist political communities. Another important step the United States should take is to lift exclusionary visa policies that have made it increasingly difficult for students from Muslim countries to attend colleges in the United States. Such policies, enacted in the aftermath of September 11, were designed to protect homeland security since some of the hijackers were registered students. However, singling out Muslim students for special restrictions has not necessarily increased security. Rather, in the words of John Paden and Peter Singer, it has "stoked the belief that the U.S. is hostile to Muslims in general" and made it more difficult for communication between young people in the Islamic world and those in the United States to occur.[43] Not long ago, the Turkish novelist Orham Pamuk, when asked what motivated an old man in Istanbul to say he approved of the September 11 attacks or a Pakistani boy to admire the Taliban, responded: "It is the feeling of impotence arising from degradation, the failure to be understood, and the inability of such people to make their voices heard."[44]

Conclusion

The evidence from this study of transnational terrorism does not support the view of Ralph Peters that we can kill our way out of the problem[45] or that reliance on force alone is an effective means of reducing transnational terrorism. At the outset of this book, I used the example of Jimmy Connors' famous tennis match against Arthur Ashe. Connors used force well. Indeed, it could be said that like our own troops in Iraq, he produced "shock and awe," but Ashe, who had never before won such an important match, found a way to undercut his opponent's power. He moved Connors around, he changed the pace, he hit soft balls, and, every bit as importantly, he played to the crowd. A frustrated Connors pumped his fists and uttered profanities. But these antics only made things worse for the reigning champion. In the end, he lost because he had the wrong strategy.

Today, the United States is in a fight-to-die match against al Qaeda and other groups that have declared war on the United States. In this match, the United States has scored points, but it has not always wanted to keep the score. To the extent that it fails to keep track of its opponents' attacks and continues to emphasize hard force at the expense of other strategies, it is unlikely to win. The United States needs to keep the score in this match (by regularly examining the impact of its strategies and tactics on its opponents' ability to mount attacks and play to a world audience). It may also need to mix up its tactics. With hard power alone, it is unlikely to succeed. With a mix of hard and soft power, and with restraints on the kind of profane and barbaric behavior that occurred at Abu Ghraib, it can still prevail.

APPENDICES

APPENDIX A:
VARIABLES IN THE ORDER OF APPEARANCE IN TEXT

Onset of War on Terrorism

Dummy variable for the start of the War on Terrorism. Coded as "0" from the first quarter of 1993 through the third quarter of 2001 and as "1" from the fourth quarter of 2001 through the fourth quarter of 2004.

Invasion of Iraq

Dummy variable for the start of the War in Iraq. Coded as "0" from the first quarter of 1993 through the first quarter of 2003 and as "1" from the second quarter of 2003 through the fourth quarter of 2004.

Capture of Saddam Hussein

Dummy variable for the timing of the capture of Iraq's former dictator, Saddam Hussein. Coded as "0" from the first quarter of 1993 through the fourth quarter of 2003 and as "1" from the first quarter of 2004 through the fourth quarter of 2004.

Release of Photos From Abu Ghraib

Dummy variable for the timing of the release of photos of U.S. soldiers abusing Iraqis at the Abu Ghraib prison. Coded as "0" from the first quarter of 1993 through the first quarter of 2004 and as "1" from the second quarter of 2004 through the fourth quarter of 2004.

Number of Incidents (a Measure of Frequency)
Log of the number of quarterly transnational terrorist incidents from January 1, 1993, through December 31, 1993. Duplicate incidents excluded for analyses of overall characteristics of incidents, time series analyses, and comparisons of unique and overlapping incidents.

Number of Days of Activity (a Measure of Frequency)
Log of the quarterly number of days on which transnational terrorist incidents were observed to occur from January 1, 1993, through December 31, 2004.

Number of Countries (a Measure of Dispersion)
Log of quarterly number of countries in which transnational terrorist incidents were observed to occur from January 1, 1993, through December 31, 2004. To standardize the databases, I collapsed incidents that were located in "disputed territories" such as Kashmir, Chechnya, and the Occupied Territories into their official countries of record. However, since both databases (RAND and ITERATE) treated Northern Ireland as a separate territory, I left that territory intact.

Number of Incidents in Countries
With 50% or Greater Muslim Populations
(a Measure of Dispersion)
Log of quarterly number of incidents in countries with 50% or greater Muslim populations from January 1, 1993, through December 31, 2004. Classification based on Wikipedia table available at http://en.wikipedia.org/wiki/Islam_by_country. This table of countries by percent Muslim population was built using the U.S. State Department's International Religious Freedom Report 2004, as well as the CIA Factbook and adherents.com. The 41 countries that met this criterion are listed in Appendix B.

Percentage of Incidents in Countries
With 50% or Greater Muslim Populations
(a Measure of Dispersion)

Percentage of quarterly number of incidents in countries with 50% or greater Muslim populations from January 1, 1993, through December 31, 2004. Classification based on Wikipedia table available at http://en.wikipedia.org/wiki/Islam_by_country. This table of countries by percent Muslim population was built using the U.S. State Department's International Religious Freedom Report 2004, as well as the CIA Factbook and adherents.com. The 41 countries that met this criterion in the dataset are listed in Appendix B.

Number of Incidents in the Middle East
and North African Region (a Measure of Dispersion)

Log of quarterly number of incidents in the 21 countries classified by the World Bank as located in the Middle East and North African region. These countries are Algeria, Bahrain, Djibouti, Egypt, Iran, Iraq, Israel, Jordan, Kuwait, Lebanon, Libya, Malta, Morocco, Oman, Qatar, Saudi Arabia, Syria, Tunisia, UAE, West Bank/Gaza, and Yemen. See "Countries and Groups," available at http://worldbank.org

Number of Deadly Incidents (a Measure of Lethality)

Log of quarterly number of incidents associated with one or more deaths of victims from January 1, 1993, through December 31, 2004. Incidents in which only a perpetrator died (as when trying to explode a bomb or when shot by police) not counted.

Number of Incidents With Deaths or Injuries
(a Measure of Lethality)

Log of quarterly number of incidents associated with one or more deaths or injuries of victims from January 1, 1993, through December 31, 2004. Incidents in which only a perpetrator died or was injured (as when trying to explode a bomb or when shot by police) not counted.

Percent Bombings (a Measure of Type of Attack)

Percent share of all incidents that could be classified as bombings from January 1, 1993, through December 31, 2004. This variable included incidents listed as explosive bombings, incendiary or fire-bombings, car bombings, suicide bombings, and letter bombings.

Percent Hostage Takings (a Measure of Type of Attack)

Percent share of all incidents that could be classified as hostage takings from January 1, 1993, through December 31, 2004. This variable included incidents listed as kidnappings, barricade and hostage seizures, and aerial hijackings involving hostages.

Number of Assassinations (a Measure of Type of Attack)

Percent share of all incidents that were classified as assassinations from January 1, 1993, through December 31, 2004. Both databases used this classification.

Incidents With Multinational Victims (a Measure of Type of Victim)

Log of quarterly number of incidents in which the victims were multinational businesses or international organizations (e.g., Red Cross, Doctors Without Borders, a UN agency) or in which the victims had more than one nationality (e.g., a local and a foreigner were injured or foreigners from more than one country were killed or injured) from January 1, 1993, through December 31, 2004. (I defined a multinational business as one that was not strictly local. McDonalds, Shell, and Nissan qualified under this definition, but a local business in Turkey did not.)

"Islamist" Perpetrated Incidents

Log of quarterly number of incidents claimed by or attributed to terrorist groups I classified as "Islamist" or "Islamist national separatist." A listing of the groups I classified as such is provided in Appendix C. As explained in the text, I did not classify secular national separatist groups such as Al Fatah or the PLO in this grouping. I did classify groups such as Al Qaeda, Hamas, and Palestinian Islamic Jihad, as well as new groupings such as the Islamic Army in Iraq and Tawid and Jihad.

APPENDIX B:
COUNTRIES CLASSIFIED 50% OR MORE MUSLIM IN DATA SET

Country	No. of Incidents
Afghanistan	121
Albania	17
Algeria	90
Azerbaijan	5
Bahrain	22
Bangladesh	6
Chad	2
Djoubiti	3
Dubai	1
Egypt	80
Equatorial Guinea	1
Eritrea	6
Ethiopia	20
Guinea (Republic)	2
Indonesia	56
Iran	28
Iraq	355
Jordan	31
Kuwait	24
Kyrgyzstan	10
Lebanon	84
Libya	1
Malaysia	4
Mali	3
Morocco	13
Niger	3

(continued)

Country	No. of Incidents
Nigeria	35
Pakistan	124
Qatar	2
Saudi Arabia	55
Senegal	1
Sierra Leone	43
Somalia	131
Sudan	31
Syria	4
Tajikistan	49
Tunisia	3
Turkey	129
UAE	2
Uzbekistan	2
Yemen	96
Total	1,695

APPENDIX C:
CLASSIFICATION OF "ISLAMIST" TERRORIST GROUPS

Name of Group	No. of Incidents
Abu Bakr al-Siddig Fundamentalist Brigades	1
Abu Sayyaf Group Philippines	28
Ahmad Qasir Martyr Group	1
Al Qaeda	67
Al Qaeda Affiliate	1
Al Qaeda_Zarquawi	1
Al Tawhid Palestinian	1
Algerian Fundamentalists	26
Algerian Islamic Salvation	1
Algerian Salvation Islamic Army	1
Ansar Allah	1
Ansar al Islam	1
Ansar al-Din	1
Ansar al-Sunnah	2
Ansar'e Hizballah Iran	1
Armed Islamic Group France	1
Armed Islamic Group GIA	43
Armed Resistance Group Mali	2
Army of Muslims	1
Assirat-al Moustaquim	5
Basics of Islam	1
Battalions of Faith	1
Brigades of the Victorious Lion of God	1
Chechen Activists/Rebels	31
Chinese Muslims	2
Dar Al Islam Western Front	1

(continued)

Name of Group	No. of Incidents
Death Squad of Iraqi Resistance	1
Divine Wrath Brigades	2
East Turkestan Liberation Organization	2
Free Aceh Movement (GAM)	4
Front for Defenders of Islam	1
GIA Genera Command Algeria	6
Global Intifada	2
Guardians of the Friend of the Prophet	1
Hamas	88
Harakat ul-Mujahadeen HuM	3
Harakat-e Enqelabe Eslami	1
Harakat-ul-Ansar	6
Harakat-ul-Jehad Islami and Asif Raza Commandos	1
Harakat-ul-Jihad Islami HUJI	1
Harakata al Intilaqah	1
Hezbollah	47
IPS People's Strugglers Mujahiddin e Kha	3
Indeterminate Afghan mujaadeen	12
Indeterminate Arab/Palestinian Guerillas	1
Indeterminate Bangladeshi Muslims	1
Indeterminate Kashmiri Nationalists	2
International Justice Group	1
Iraqi Legitimate Resistance	1
Isaami Harakut-ul Mominem	1
Islamic Army in Iraq	13
Islamic Front for Liberation of Bahrain	2
Islamic Jihad Against Oppressors	1
Islamic Jihad Brigades	1

(continued)

CLASSIFICATION OF "ISLAMIST" TERRORIST GROUPS
(continued)

Name of Group	No. of Incidents
Islamic Jihad Cells Lebanon	1
Islamic Jihad Organization	9
Islamic Jihad Yemen	1
Islamic Movement Iranian Sunni	1
Islamic Movement of Iraqi Mujahideen	2
Islamic Movement of Martyrs Cyprus	1
Islamic Preaching Group	1
Islamic Renewal Group	1
Islamic Resistance Brigades	2
Islamic Revival Movement Tajikistan	2
Islamic Union Somalia	3
Izz-al-Din al Qassam Brigades	3
JI Jemaah Islamiyah	8
Jaish-e-Mohammad (JeM)	1
Jami at-e Eslami	1
Jammu and Kashmir Islamic Front	3
Jemoat	1
Jihad Brigades	1
Jordanian Islamic Resistance	1
KHAD Secret Service Afg	1
Karbala Brigades	1
Kurdish Islamic Unity Party	1
Lashkar-e-Jabbar (LeJ)	1
Lashkar-eTaiba (LeT)	5
Lashkar-i-Jhangvi	1
Laskar-I-taiba Pakistan	2
Liberation Party	1

(continued)

Name of Group	No. of Incidents
Libyan agents	1
Likah Asept al-Islamiya	1
Lions of Allah Brigade	2
MILF Moro Islamic National Liberation Front	8
MLF Moro National Liberation Front	5
Mahdi Army	1
Movement for Islamic Change	4
Movement for the Struggle of the Jordanian Islamic	2
Mujaheddin Army	1
Mujahideen Brigades	1
Mujahidin Division Khandaq	1
Mullah Salam	1
Muslim United Army	23
Muslim Yaqub Momen	1
Muzolokandov's Gang Islamic Group Tajikistan	2
Palestinian Islamic Jihad (PLJ)	29
Pathan Tribe Afghanistan	1
Pattani United Liberation	2
Popular Front for Liberation of Palestine (PFLP)	1
Pro-Mujib Force	1
Qaeda al-Jihad	1
Revolution of the 1920s Brigade	1
Salafi Abu-Bakr al-Siddiq Grou	1
Salafist Group	3
Salafist Group GSPC	7
Saraya Usud al-Tawhid	1
Saudi Hizbollah	1
Shi'ite Muslim Activists	8
Students of Musa Abu Marzuq	1

(continued)

CLASSIFICATION OF "ISLAMIST" TERRORIST GROUPS
(continued)

Name of Group	No. of Incidents
Sunni Muslim Warriors Pakistan	1
Takfir wa Hijah Sudan	2
Talai al Fath Egypt	4
Taliban	32
Tanzim Qa'idat Al-Jihad fi Bilad al-Rafidayn	1
Tawhid and Jihad	12
Thawart al-Ishrin Brigades	1
The Holders of the Black Banners	1
The Muslim Group Egypt	25
Turkish Islamic Jihad	1
Union of Imams	1
Unknown Group (attribution to Islamist activists)	11
Western Trace Islamists	1
al Jame'ah of Int'l Justice	1
al-Dali Group Algeria	1
al-Faran	3
al-Gama'a al-Islamiyya (GAI)	17
al-Hadid	3
al-Hugban Operatkon Martyr's Group Islamic Resistance	1
al-Zarqawi group	6
Total	722

APPENDIX D:
EXPLANATION OF REGRESSION OUTPUT

The table provided, Table D1, is composed of a series of subtables. The first subtable shows the results of a least squares regression for the effect of time (indicated as "quarter number") on the dependent variable of interest. The R-square or coefficient of determination indicates the amount of variance explained by this variable as a fraction.[1] The F-test indicates whether there is a statistically significant change in the series over time. This subtable also provides the Durbin–Watson statistic—a measure that assesses if a series has autocorrelation. It is important to remove autocorrelation in time series because autocorrelation can bias or confound results. In general, a Durbin–Watson statistic that is close to "2" is desirable. In the first subtable in Table D1, the Durbin–Watson statistic is 1.18, indicating that the series has autocorrelation.

The next subtable provides a graphic depiction of the autocorrelation in the series at different lags or intervals. For Number of Incidents (Table D1), serial dependence (autocorrelation) is problematic for the first two lags (meaning an observation in Quarter 4 is likely to be dependent on observations in Quarters 3 and 2, and an observation in Quarter 28 is likely to be dependent on observations in Quarters 27 and 26). Although autocorrelation at other lags exists, the values for the autocorrelation coefficients (AC) and partial autocorrelation coefficients are highest for the first two lags. Since the regression I plan requires the removal of autocorrelation, I build an ARIMA model to take out this serial dependency.

The last subtable provides a least squares multiple regression of the effect of time and the other independent variables (the onset of the War on Terrorism, the start of the War in Iraq, the Capture of Saddam Hussein) *after* an ARIMA model has been fitted to take out autocorrelation. This subtable provides the Durbin–Watson statistic after the ARIMA model is run. In Table D1, the Durbin–Watson is now close to 2 as it should be for a regression. Another F-test is provided. This F-test is used to test whether the combination of time and the independent variables of interest are associated with a significant overall change in the dependent variable of interest, in this case the number of incidents. This subtable also provides the coefficients for each of the independent variables after the regression has been run. The coefficients indicate the fraction or percentage contribution of each independent variable to change in the series when the other independent variables and time are held constant.[2] In Table D1, the coefficient for the Global War on Terrorism (GWOT) is 0.735. This can be interpreted to mean that, controlling for time and the other independent variables, the GWOT is associated with a 73% increase in transnational terrorist incidents over and above the average number of incidents in the period before the GWOT. The t-test tests the significance of each coefficient. In Table D1, the probability that the coefficient (0.735) for the GWOT is significant is .0001. We reject the null hypothesis of no significant effect and accept the alternative hypothesis that the GWOT increased transnational terrorist incidents. For this measure, the coefficient for Abu Ghraib is also significant. On the other hand, although the invasion of Iraq has a coefficient of 0.265 (indicating that it was associated with a 26% increase in incidents), this coefficient is not statistically significant. (In some cases, high coefficients are not statistically significant because the effect is not a smooth or consistent one.)

Table D1. Number of incidents.

Dependent Variable: LOG(INCIDENTS)
Method: Least Squares
Date: 12/04/05 Time: 11:23
Sample: 1993:1 2004:4
Included observations: 48

Variable	Coefficient	Std. Error	t-Statistic	Prob.
QUARTER_NUMBER 01	–0.010904	0.004359	–2.501850	0.0160
C	4.763061	0.122672	38.82757	0.0000

R-squared	0.119773	Mean dependent var	4.495905
Adjusted R-squared	0.100638	S.D. dependent var	0.441110
S.E. of regression	0.418326	Akaike info criterion	1.135661
Sum squared resid	8.049837	Schwarz criterion	1.213628
Log likelihood	–25.25587	F-statistic	6.259251
Durbin–Watson stat	1.186148	Prob(F-statistic)	0.015974

Date: 12/04/05 Time: 11:24
Sample: 1993:1 2004:4
Included observations: 48

Autocorrelation	Partial Correlation		AC	PAC	Q-Stat	Prob
. |*** |	. |*** |	1	0.375	0.375	7.1751	0.007
. |** |	. |** |	2	0.320	0.209	12.525	0.002
. |*. |	. | . |	3	0.160	–0.016	13.899	0.003
. |** |	. |*. |	4	0.256	0.177	17.469	0.002
. |** |	. |*. |	5	0.290	0.176	22.172	0.000
. |** |	. | . |	6	0.227	0.014	25.117	0.000
. | . |	.*| . |	7	0.044	–0.163	25.232	0.001
.*| . |	.*| . |	8	–0.074	–0.171	25.561	0.001
. | . |	. |*. |	9	0.043	0.087	25.675	0.002
. |** |	. |** |	10	0.235	0.268	29.166	0.001
. | . |	.*| . |	11	0.057	–0.147	29.377	0.002
. | . |	.*| . |	12	–0.039	–0.145	29.477	0.003

(continued)

Table D1. *(continued)* Number of incidents.

Autocorrelation	Partial Correlation		AC	PAC	Q-Stat	Prob
.*| . |	. | . |	13	–0.125	–0.011	30.548	0.004
.*| . |	.*| . |	14	–0.123	–0.088	31.611	0.005
.*| . |	**| . |	15	–0.125	–0.203	32.754	0.005
.*| . |	. | . |	16	–0.072	–0.015	33.138	0.007
**| . |	.*| . |	17	–0.285	–0.138	39.417	0.002
***| . |	.*| . |	18	–0.390	–0.183	51.589	0.000
**| . |	. |*. |	19	–0.238	0.084	56.263	0.000
.*| . |	. | . |	20	–0.180	–0.019	59.037	0.000

Dependent Variable: LOG(INCIDENTS)
Method: Least Squares
Date: 12/04/05 Time: 11:25
Sample(adjusted): 1993:3 2004:4
Included observations: 46 after adjusting endpoints
Convergence achieved after three iterations

Variable	Coefficient	Std. Error	t-Statistic	Prob.
QUARTER_NUMBER01	–0.000238	0.010588	–0.022456	0.9822
C	4.447742	0.321371	13.83988	0.0000
AR(1)	0.284875	0.142120	2.004466	0.0515
AR(2)	0.277470	0.147321	1.883444	0.0666

R-squared	0.265214	Mean dependent var	4.461254
Adjusted R-squared	0.212729	S.D. dependent var	0.411728
S.E. of regression	0.365319	Akaike info criterion	0.906850
Sum squared resid	5.605235	Schwarz criterion	1.065862
Log likelihood	–16.85754	F-statistic	5.053166
Durbin–Watson stat	2.001780	Prob(F-statistic)	0.004442

Inverted AR Roots	.69	–.40	

(continued)

Table D1. *(continued)* Number of incidents.

Dependent Variable: LOG(INCIDENTS)
Method: Least Squares
Date: 12/04/05 Time: 11:26
Sample(adjusted): 1993:3 2004:4
Included observations: 46 after adjusting endpoints
Convergence achieved after eight iterations

Variable	Coefficient	Std. Error	t-Statistic	Prob.
EVENT_PHOTOS_AB U_GRAIHIB	1.096846	0.366423	2.993385	0.0048
EVENT_TIME_CAPT URE_SH01	−0.774074	0.381279	−2.030203	0.0494
EVENT_TIME_GWOT 01	0.735248	0.162177	4.533613	0.0001
EVENT_TIME_WAR_ IRAQ01	0.265559	0.213961	1.241152	0.2222
QUARTER_NUMBER 01	−0.032541	0.005186	−6.274523	0.0000
C	5.039608	0.109489	46.02865	0.0000
AR(1)	−0.075582	0.157175	−0.480880	0.6334
AR(2)	−0.029314	0.168109	−0.174372	0.8625

R-squared	0.533041	Mean dependent var	4.461254
Adjusted R-squared	0.447023	S.D. dependent var	0.411728
S.E. of regression	0.306171	Akaike info criterion	0.627424
Sum squared resid	3.562144	Schwarz criterion	0.945449
Log likelihood	−6.430762	F-statistic	6.196805
Durbin–Watson stat	2.001705	Prob(F-statistic)	0.000071

Inverted AR Roots	−.04 −.17i	−.04+.17i

APPENDIX E:
ITERATE AND RAND COMPARED

The ITERATE database contained a total of 2,854 transnational terrorist incidents for the study period. The RAND database had a remarkably close total number of such incidents, 2,742 for the same period. To the casual observer, this similarity might suggest that the two databases captured the same incidents. However, as was pointed out earlier, only about 30% of incidents in each database were duplicates of incidents in the other database.

When incidents across the two databases were compared, several significant differences were observed. These differences, described next, highlight the importance of using more than one source to gain a more comprehensive data set.

As shown in Figure E1, there were distinct differences in the regional distribution of incidents. Although the distribution was

Figure E1. Comparison of ITERATE and RAND: Percent distribution of transnational terrorist incidents by World Bank region of occurrence, 1993–2004.

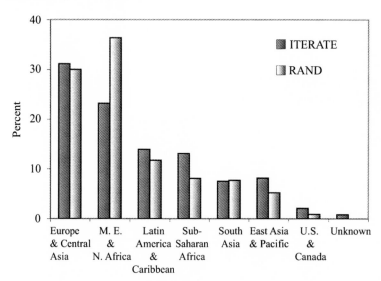

similar for Europe and Central Asia and for South Asia, RAND had a larger concentration of incidents in the Middle East and North African region (36% vs. 23%). Conversely, ITERATE had larger concentrations in Latin America (14% vs. 12%), Sub-Saharan Africa (13% vs. 9%), East Asia (8% vs. 5%), and the U.S./Canada region (2% vs. 1%). These regional differences were statistically significant (chi-square = 186, *df* = 7, *p* < .001).[3]

Closer inspection of the incidents by country suggests that the two databases are likely to have tapped into different information in different countries even within the same regions. As noted earlier, 24 countries with 50 or more incidents over the study period were responsible for more than three fourths of all incidents in each of the databases (77% in ITERATE and 76% in RAND).

As shown in Figure E2, the country distribution of incidents was similar in the South Asian region (where the countries with the largest numbers of incidents were Afghanistan, Pakistan, and India) and in the Sub-Saharan African region (where the countries with the highest number of incidents were Sierra Leone, Angola, and Nigeria). However, in the Middle East and North Africa region, incidents in Israel and its Occupied Territories made up as much as 16% of all incidents in the RAND database compared with only 3% in ITERATE. In other words, compared with ITERATE, the RAND database had five times as high a percentage of incidents occurring in Israel and the Occupied Territories.

Other differences in the country distribution of incidents in the Middle East and North Africa were also observed. For example, RAND had a slightly higher percentage than ITERATE of incidents in Iraq (9% vs. 6%) and Turkey (3.6% vs. 2.1%). On the other hand, ITERATE had slightly higher percentages of incidents than RAND in Somalia (3.8% vs. 1.7%), Yemen (2.6% vs. 1.8%), Algeria (2.5% vs. 2.2%), and Egypt (2.2% vs. 1.6%).

Figure E2. Comparison of ITERATE and RAND: Percent distribution of transnational terrorist incidents by country of occurrence for the 32 countries with the highest number of incidents, 1993–2004.

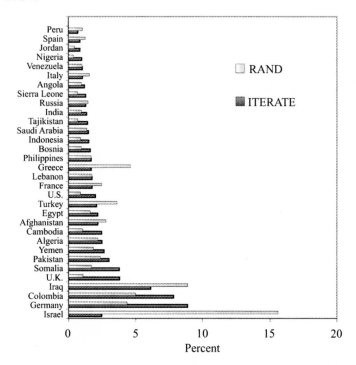

There were also differences in the Europe and Central Asia region where RAND had a higher concentration of incidents in Greece (4.6% vs. 1.7%), whereas ITERATE had higher concentrations in Germany (8.9% vs. 4.3%) and the United Kingdom (3.8% vs. 1.1%). In addition, the two databases also showed differences in the Latin American region where Colombia contributed 7.8% of all incidents in the ITERATE database but only 5% of incidents in RAND.

Since transnational terrorism, after September 11, has come to be associated with Islamist terrorism in the popular mind and since countries with large Muslim populations have witnessed a considerable share of transnational terrorism, I also compared the two databases in terms of the percentage distribution of incidents in predominantly Muslim countries (Figure E3). This analysis indicated a small but statistically higher percentage of incidents in predominantly Muslim countries in ITERATE compared with RAND (40% vs. 37%, chi-square = 6.38, $df = 1, p < .02$).

I also examined database differences in numbers of incidents over time. The average number of total incidents per quarter (3-month interval) for the study period ranged from 10 to 243 for ITERATE and from 11 to 119 for RAND. The median number of incidents per quarter was remarkably similar: 55 for ITERATE and 57.5 for RAND. Visual inspection of the two time series over time, however (Figure E4), indicates that ITERATE had a higher number of

Figure E3. Comparison of ITERATE and RAND: Percent distribution of transnational terrorist incidents by percent Muslim population, 1993–2004.

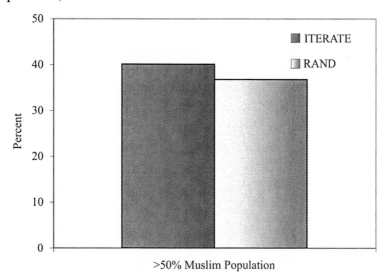

Figure E4. Comparison of ITERATE and RAND: Number of transnational terrorist incidents by year, 1993–2004 (all incidents).

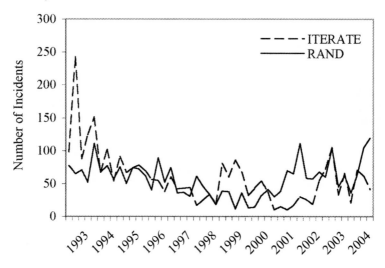

incidents in early 1993 and 1994, a period that coincided with the breakup of the former Soviet Union. On the other hand, RAND had a higher number of incidents in late 2001 and 2002, as well as in the latter part of 2004. These differences are likely to have been a function of two processes: (1) greater capture by ITERATE of incidents in Europe in the early 1990s and (2) greater capture by RAND of incidents in Israel and the Occupied Territories during the Intifada and of incidents in Iraq during the second year of the War in Iraq. As shown in Figure E5, when Israel was excluded, the numbers of incidents for the first 2 years of the millennium show closer correspondence.

The most common types of incidents, accounting for 83% of incidents in ITERATE and 92% in RAND, involved (1) bombings (including explosive bombings, car bombings, fire bombings, letter bombings, and suicide bombings); (2) hostage events (including

Figure E5. Comparison of ITERATE and RAND: Number of transnational terrorist incidents, 1993–2004 (Israel excluded).

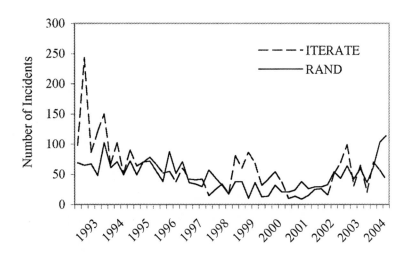

kidnappings, barricade hostage events, skyjackings, and occupation of facilities); (3) armed attacks (e.g., missile attacks, as well as attacks with rifles, guns, knives, or other weapons); (4) assassinations (usually so classified because they involved the killing of an official); and (5) threats, a category that featured in ITERATE but not in RAND.

Comparison of the percentage distribution of these types of incidents indicated differences only for bombings and threats. As shown in Figure E6, bombings accounted for 43% of all incidents by type of attack in RAND compared with only 27% in ITERATE. This difference was statistically significant (chi-square = 5.77, $df = 1$, $p < .025$). On the other hand, the percentages of incidents classified as hostage events, armed attacks, and assassinations were similar and not statistically different across the two databases. It is likely that the lower percentage of bombings in ITERATE is a function of its inclusion in its database of incidents classified as "threats" and its inclusion of a category called "other actions,"

Figure E6. Comparison of ITERATE and RAND: Percent distribution of transnational terrorist incidents by type of attack, 1993–2004.

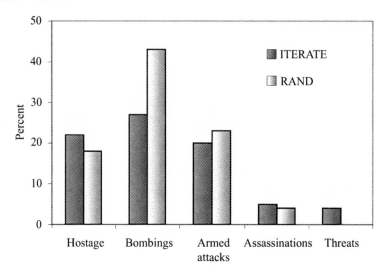

each contributing 7% to the total. In some cases, RAND incidents classified as "bombings" might have been classified in the threat category in ITERATE (e.g., if the bombing stopped before it was initiated or it was intercepted). Also, some incidents classified as "other actions" by ITERATE might have been placed in the bombing or armed attack category by RAND.

I also compared the two databases by lethality of attack. Figure E7 shows that deadly attacks constituted 28% of all attacks in ITERATE and 31% of all attacks in the RAND database. This difference, although small, was statistically significant (chi-square = 5.9, $df = 1, p < .015$). In addition, there was a statistically significant difference between the sources in the number of incidents with deaths *or* injuries (chi-square = 18.1, $df = 1, p < .0001$). Again, RAND had a slightly higher percentage of such incidents compared with ITERATE (43% vs. 37%). These differences may be a

Figure E7. Comparison of ITERATE and RAND: Percent distribution of transnational terrorist incidents by lethality, 1993–2004.

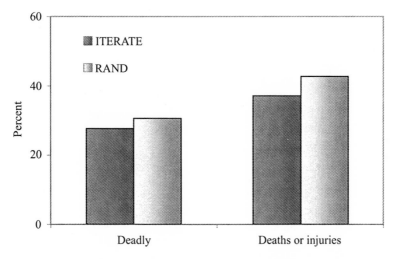

function of the larger number of nonfatal, noninjurious incidents in Europe in ITERATE. They may also be related to the inclusion in ITERATE of as many as 186 incidents that were classified in the "threat" category and by definition were not associated with deaths or injuries.

In both databases, incidents in which private parties (including missionaries, tourists, students, and other private citizens) and private property were the immediate victims were more common than incidents involving other types of victims (Figure E8). For ITERATE, the percentage of incidents with the immediate victim classified as one or more private citizens or property was 41.1%. For RAND, the percentage was remarkably similar, 39.5%. The percentage of attacks classified as being against foreign diplomats was also very similar (18.3% for ITERATE and 18.9% for RAND).

On the other hand, a somewhat larger proportion of RAND incidents, compared with ITERATE, involved victims classified

Figure E8. Comparison of ITERATE and RAND: Percent distribution of transnational terrorist incidents by type of immediate victim, 1993–2004.

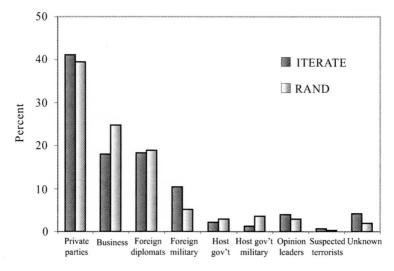

as businesspersons or property (25% vs. 18%) and victims classified as host government military (3.5% vs. 1%). Conversely, a larger percentage of ITERATE incidents, compared with RAND, involved victims classified as foreign military (10% vs. 5%). These differences, which proved to be statistically significant when chi-square was applied to the overall comparison (chi-square = 150, $df = 8$, $p < .0001$),[4] may have reflected a somewhat greater focus by RAND on incidents against businesses and by ITERATE on incidents involving foreign troops, for example, NATO troops in Eastern Europe. It is also likely that the slightly higher percentage of incidents relating to host government military in the RAND database is a function of its inclusion of more incidents from Israel and the Occupied Territories. Such incidents, to be transnational, would have had to involve a foreign national, for example, a Syrian or Lebanese mounting an attack against a member of the Israeli military forces. An attack by an Israeli or by a Palestinian from the Occupied Territories would not be classified as transnational.

One or more U.S. victims (persons and or property) were present in 28.9% of the incidents in the ITERATE database and 22.5% of those in the RAND database (Figure E9). This difference, although again relatively small, was statistically significant (chi-square = 29.1, *df* = 1, *p* < .0001). Further analysis of the breakdown of incidents with U.S. victims by type of victim showed that the RAND database had a somewhat larger concentration of incidents with U.S. business victims compared with ITERATE (41.7% vs. 32.6%). On the other hand, ITERATE had a larger percentage of incidents with U.S. military victims (11.1% vs. 8.1%) and with U.S. victims classified as unknown type (4.1% vs. 1.1%).

In the two databases, almost equal percentages of incidents (37.3% for ITERATE and 36.3% for RAND) could be classified as having

Figure E9. Comparison of ITERATE and RAND: Percent distribution of transnational terrorist incidents by presence of U.S. victim, 1993–2004.

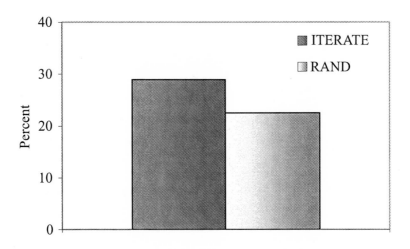

multinational victims; that is, victims from more than one country or from international organizations, for example, the UN and the Red Cross (Figure E10). Of the 1,622 incidents with multinational victims, 391 (24%) involved international organizations or members of such organizations.

For a large percentage of incidents (46% in ITERATE and 53% in RAND), the perpetrator organization was unknown and therefore impossible to classify. Using RAND's classification system for perpetrator organizations, but separating out from the category "Religious" those attacks which could be attributed to Islamist groups (such as al Qaeda or Islamist-oriented/national separatist groups such as Hamas), I looked at the distribution of incidents by type of perpetrator organization. This analysis demonstrated very little difference across the two databases. Attacks by known leftist groups (communist, socialist, and anarchist groups) constituted

Figure E10. Comparison of ITERATE and RAND: Percent distribution of transnational terrorist incidents by multinational classification of the victim(s), 1993–2004.

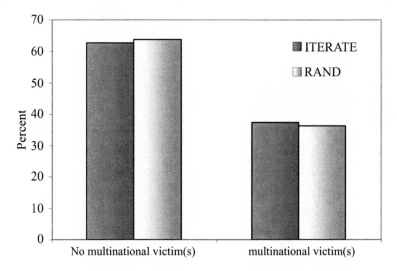

Figure E11. Comparison of ITERATE and RAND: Percent distribution of transnational terrorist incidents by type of perpetrator organization, 1993–2004.

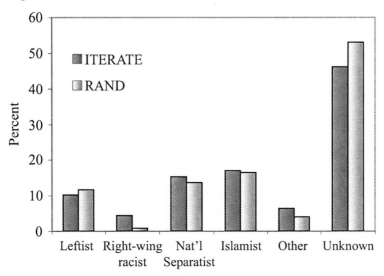

10.2% of all incidents in ITERATE and 11.7% in RAND. Attacks by right-wing or racist groups, including Neo-Nazi groups, were only slightly more common in ITERATE compared with RAND (4.4% vs. 0.8%). Nor was any large difference between the databases found in the distribution of attacks by secular national separatist groups (e.g., Irish Republican Army, Tamil Tigers, Palestine Liberation Organization), which constituted 15% of the incidents in ITERATE and 14% in RAND, or in attacks by known Islamist or Islamist national separatist groups, which made up 17% of incidents in ITERATE and 16.5% in RAND (Figure E11).

OVERLAPPING AND UNIQUE INCIDENTS

As noted, 863 incidents or about 30% of all incidents in each source replicated (duplicated) incidents in the other source. For most of the quarters in the study period (1993–2004), the ratio of unique to overlapping incidents was 3:1 or 4:1. This pattern changed from the second quarter of 1999 through the year 2000 when the number of unique incidents spiked and the ratio of unique to overlapping incidents rose from 4:1 to as high as 16:1. This shift was almost certainly related to greater coverage in RAND of transnational terrorist events associated with the Intifada occurring at that time in Israel and the Occupied Territories. The ratio of unique to overlapping incidents also increased (to 7:1) after the start of the War on Terrorism but was more consistently in the range of 3:1 from late 2002 onwards (Figure E12).

The pattern of overlapping incidents may be of special interest insofar as they shed light on agreement on transnational terrorist

Figure E12. Comparison of overlapping and unique transnational terrorist incidents in ITERATE and RAND by quarterly time period, 1993–2004.

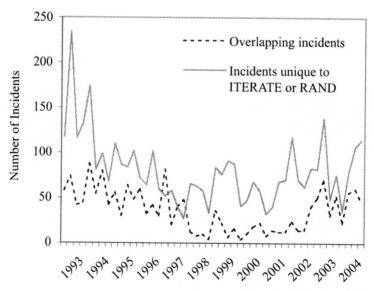

incidents or constitute a core on which observers tend to focus. Closer inspection indicated that overlapping incidents differed from unique ones in several respects.

First, overlapping incidents were more likely to be deadly. Forty-one percent of overlapping incidents compared with only 23% of unique incidents were associated with deaths. This difference was statistically significant (chi-square = 98.7, df = 1, p < .0001). Over-lapping incidents were also significantly more likely to be associated with deaths or injuries. As shown in Figure E13, 52.4% of overlapping incidents compared with only 34.2% of unique incidents were associated with deaths or injuries (chi-square = 98.8, df = 1, p < .0001).

In addition to being more lethal, overlapping incidents had a significantly different pattern of regional distribution (chi-square = 42.5, df = 6, p < .0001). As shown in Figure E14, such incidents

Figure E13. Comparison of overlapping and unique transnational terrorist incidents in ITERATE and RAND: Distribution by lethality, 1993–2004.

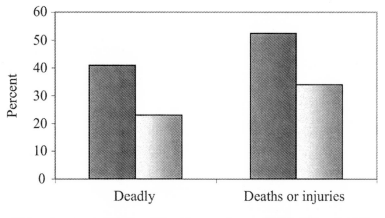

Figure E14. Comparison of overlapping and unique transnational terrorist incidents in ITERATE and RAND: Distribution by region, 1993–2004.

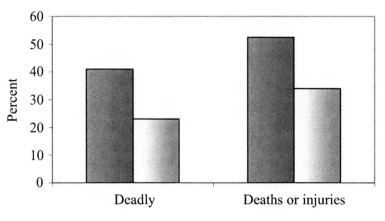

■ Overlapping incidents   ☐ Incidents unique to ITERATE or RAND

were more likely to be located in the Middle East or North Africa and less likely to be located in Europe or Central Asia.

Overlapping incidents were also more likely than unique ones to be located in countries with populations more than 50% Muslim (chi-square = 65.3, df = 1, p < .0001). As shown in Figure E15, 49% of overlapping incidents compared with only 34% of unique incidents were located in predominantly Muslim countries.

Additional differences between overlapping and unique incidents were detected for the distribution of type of attacks. Although bombings and armed attacks (e.g., attacks with rifles, guns, etc.) were equally represented, overlapping incidents had significantly larger shares of hostage takings (24.3% vs. 14.8%, chi-square = 42.8, df = 1, p < .001) and assassinations (8.9% vs. 5.4%, chi-square = 15.14, df = 1, p < .001) (Figure E16).

Overlapping incidents were also more likely to have U.S. citizens as victims. As shown, 30% of overlapping incidents but only

Figure E15. Comparison of overlapping and unique transnational terrorist incidents in ITERATE and RAND: Distribution by percent in Muslim countries, 1993–2004.

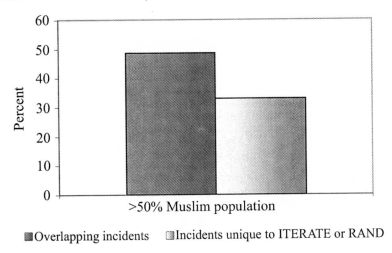

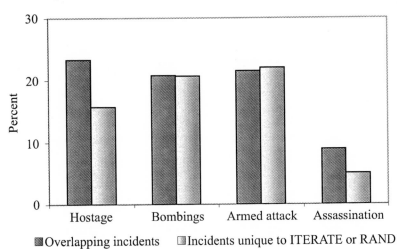

Figure E16. Comparison of overlapping and unique transnational terrorist incidents in ITERATE and RAND: Distribution by type of attack, 1993–2004.

24% of unique ones had one or more U.S. victims (chi-square = 15.3.28, $df = 1$, $p < .0001$). In addition, there was a pattern for a slightly larger proportion of overlapping incidents compared with unique ones (44% vs. 39%) to have private citizens as victims (chi-square = 9.4, $df = 1$, $p < .002$). On the other hand, overlapping incidents were not found to be any more likely than unique ones to have business victims or victims classified as diplomats (Figure E17).

Finally, overlapping incidents had a significantly higher proportion of incidents associated with known Islamist and Islamist national separatist perpetrator groups (25% vs. 13%, chi-square = 69.9, $df = 1$, $p < .0001$) and a simultaneously lower proportion of incidents of events associated with unknown perpetrators (42% vs. 53%, chi-square = 37.2, $df = 1$, $p < .0001$) (Figure E18).

Figure E17. Comparison of overlapping and unique transnational terrorist incidents in ITERATE and RAND: Distribution by type of victim, 1993–2004.

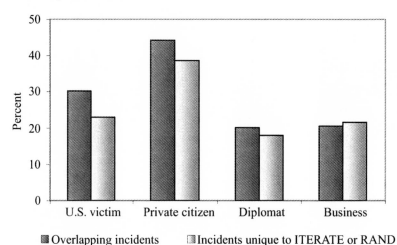

Figure E18. Comparison of overlapping and unique transnational terrorist incidents in ITERATE and RAND: Distribution by type of perpetrator group, 1993–2004.

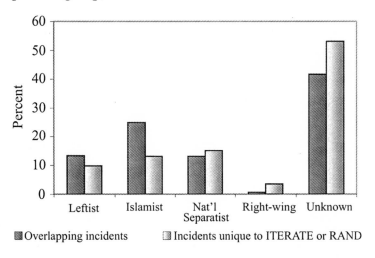

■ Overlapping incidents   ▣ Incidents unique to ITERATE or RAND

In sum, for the time period studied, overlapping incidents were more likely to be deadly, to involve hostage takings and assassinations, to occur in predominantly Muslim countries, to target private citizens, and to be perpetrated by known "Islamist" or "Islamist national separatist groups." These characteristics suggest that there may be a core of transnational terrorist incidents on which observers from different reference frames agree. The parameters of these incidents may be of special research interest for this reason. On the other hand, it is likely that because of the costly and time-consuming nature of events data collection, many incidents are simply missed in both databases. I chose to include unique, as well as overlapping, incidents in the analysis to provide as comprehensive a dataset as possible.

ENDNOTES

CHAPTER 1

1. Gray, D. (1975, July 6). On a remarkable Wimbledon. *The Guardian*.
2. Arreguin-Toft (2001, p. 96).
3. Arreguin-Toft (2001). See also Pape (2003, p. 344). Pape argues that strategy has been key in the success of suicide terrorism, which, he tallies, has been effective in about 50% of the cases in which it has been used. He notes that it was effective in compelling American and French military forces to leave Lebanon in 1983, Israeli forces to abandon Lebanon in 1985, and Israeli forces to quit the Gaza Strip and West Bank in 1994 and 1995, respectively. He also suggests that it was effective in getting the Sri Lankan government to create an independent Tamil state from 1990 on and the Turkish government to grant autonomy to Kurds in the late 1990s. See also Dershowitz (2002).
4. See Perito (2003, p. 84).
5. Slim (1998).
6. Lacina, Russett, and Gleditsch (2005). See also Hanley (2004). Hanley cites information from the International Peace Research Institute 2004 Yearbook report, a collaboration with Sweden's Uppsala University, which indicates that the number of intrastate conflicts has declined and there was also a decline in battle deaths worldwide from 400,000 to 100,000 in the 1990s to 20,000 in 2003.
7. I use the term *substate* here to refer to actors (individuals and groups) operating for the most part within a state but without official state sanction. I use the term *nonstate* to refer to actors operating for the most part outside state boundaries without official state sanction. These distinctions, however, are not as cut and dried as one might expect when it comes to politically motivated violence and terrorism. Substate actors engaged in terrorism within a state often do cross state boundaries to stage attacks. In addition, they may have or gain semiofficial status within a state as the Palestinian Liberation Organization (PLO) and Tamil Tigers did. Such actors may also have backing by an external state (as Hezbollah has had backing by Iran). Similar caveats need to be observed with regard to the term *nonstate*. Although bin Laden's al Qaeda group is generally viewed as a nonstate actor, it has operated within specific states (e.g., Sudan, Afghanistan) with the backing, if not always the official sanction, of these states.

8. Senechal de la Roche (2004, p. 3). Schmid and Jongman (1988) make a similar point

9. In a recent study in *Injury Prevention*, Nick Wilson and his colleagues found that deaths from road accidents in developed economies were 390 times higher than those from international terrorism (study available at http://www.breitbart.com/news/2005/11/30/051130231753.72wocvgo.html). It is estimated that transnational terrorism was responsible for about 300 deaths per year in the 1990s and that domestic terrorism was responsible for about 3,000 deaths per year. In contrast, data from the Armed Conflict and Intervention Project at the University of Maryland's CIDCM indicates that there were about 300,000 deaths per year in the 1990s in interstate and intrastate wars. See Marshall (2002).

10. See Jentleson (2002). He notes the relative paucity of research on terror-related topics in the International Relations field prior to September 11 and the degree to which research agendas in this area have suffered from "a degree of marginality." See also Cronin (2002/2003), who observes that "it has been alleged that a principal interest in terrorism virtually guarantees exclusion from most academic positions." She points out that a few major scholars such as Martha Crenshaw and Paul Wilkinson have shown an interest in the strategic meanings of terrorism for over three decades. In addition, over the past 15 years, Enders and Sandler have put their considerable econometric expertise to the arduous task of understanding the effects of a variety of policies on terrorist tactics and strategies, and more recently, Pape has turned his attention to the "strategic logic" of one tactic, suicide terrorism. Still, much of the work focusing on the dynamics and outcomes of terrorism was left to think tanks. As Cronin points out, although resident scholars such as Walter Laqueur (CSIS), Bruce Hoffman (RAND), and Paul Pillar in the intelligence community have all produced important insights, the institutions themselves are all too often limited by "narrow interests and short time frames of government contracts on which they depend." According to Lake (2003), intrastate (civil) war was also marginalized by scholars in the international relations field.

11. See Rubenstein (2003).

12. Although factors such as poverty and lack of education have long been identified as causal factors, empirical evidence indicates that individuals who engage in terrorism tend to have more rather than fewer economic resources than others in their own communities and also have higher levels of education and occupation. See Krueger (2003) and Krueger and Maleckova (2003a, 2003b). For more empirical evidence, see Berrebi (2003). For further discussion of the link between poverty, education, and terrorism, see USAID (2002), Pion-Berlin (1984), Zwick (2004), Enders, Sandler, and Parise (1992), Enders, Sandler, and Cauley (1990), and Enders and Sandler (2000).

13. Scholars such as Wiktorowicz (2001, 2004) of Yale are beginning to remedy this inattention in relation to Islamist extremist violence, but more needs to be done.

14. Throughout this book and in the figures, GWOT will be used to refer to the Global War on Terrorism.

15. The term *strategy* is used here to refer to an actor's plan for using military forces to achieve political objectives. The term *tactics* is used to refer to the means.

16. The term *preemption* has been defined as striking an enemy as it prepares to strike. However, some observers have suggested that the Bush administration has expanded the definition to include "prevention," that is, striking an enemy even in the absence of specific evidence of an imminent attack. See O'Hanlon, Rice and Steinberg (2002). This interpretation is consistent with the words of President Bush in the days immediately after the September 11 attack: "Our war on terror begins with al Qaeda, but it does not end there. It will not end until every terrorist group of global reach has been found, stopped, and defeated." See Bush (2001).

17. See Lake (2002).

18. According to a 2002 United Nations report, al Qaeda recruitment picked up in 30 to 40 countries during the period the United States began building up for the Iraq invasion (see Lynch, 2002). According to a CSIS report, interviews of foreign fighters in Iraq indicated that images of abuse at Abu Ghraib were an important catalyst in their decision to fight (see Obaid & Cordesman, 2005).

19. See Della Porta (1996, p. 95). See also Hamilton and Hamilton (1983).

20. See Lichbach (1987). See also as cited in Lichbach: Zimmerman (1980), Opp and Roehl (1990), and Rasler (1996).

21. See Bueno de Mesquita (2003).

22. See Enders and Sandler (1993).

23. See Lichbach (1987).

24. See Lichbach (1987).

25. Greene (1984), cited in Lichbach (1987, p. 269).

26. See Mack (1975). See also Schelling (1963).

27. "What Next for U.S. Foreign Policy?" Interview with Ralph Peters, June 2003, available at http://www.reason.com/0306/fe.jw.what.shtml

28. Rational choice models, based on bargaining theory, posit that war is an inefficient and suboptimal outcome since, as Fearon has put it, under most conditions, bargains exist that rational adversaries "would prefer to a risky and costly fight." Fearon argues that war occurs when misinformation or miscalculation of an adversary's power, will, or resources leads to a bargaining failure. According to this model, which has been extended to civil war and terrorism,

combat helps both sides improve information and thus leads to capitulation, settlement, or shifts into lower level violence. See Fearon (1995). See also Overgaard (1994) and Lichbach (2005).

29. See Arreguin-Toft (2001, p. 106).

30. Lake (2002, p. 18) argues that terrorist groups should not be viewed as unitary actors but rather in terms of "concentric rings" that include social-movement radicals (who share goals), sympathizers (who provide active support, such as apartments), and actual terrorists (who carry out violence). He places moderates outside these groups but suggests that terrorism is designed to shift populations "from one ring to another, that is, moderates into social-movement radicals, radicals into sympathizers, sympathizers into terrorists."

31. See Pruitt and Rubin (1986, p. 64).

32. See Rubin, Pruitt, and Kim (1986).

33. See Sandole (1993).

34. Time series intervention analyses, also called "interrupted time series" analyses, are often used to evaluate the impact of a key event on a series of observations.

35. Previous published quantitative analyses of transnational terrorism have been limited almost exclusively to one proprietary database (ITERATE originally compiled by CIA analyst Edward Mickolus (1980, 1982, 1993) and updated by Mickolus, Sandler and Murdock (1989), Mickolus and Simmons (1997, 2002) and by Mickolus, Sandler, Murdock and Fleming (2003). My own analysis of several years of ITERATE, however, indicates that it misses many items that fit its own definition of transnational terrorism and are covered in the text-based RAND–MIPT database originally compiled by terrorism experts, Brian Jenkins and Bruce Hoffman, and now available at the MIPT Memorial Institute for the Prevention of Terrorism http://www.tkb.org. To make up for this short-fall, I supplement the ITERATE data set with RAND–MIPT data (which I have coded following the ITERATE format). To my knowledge, no one has used the RAND dataset for quantitative analyses because, although it has recently been made available on the web, it is only available in text format and coding is time consuming. Other databases also exist. In particular, the U.S. Department of State (1996–2003) compiles an annual series of transnational terrorist events. However, this dataset is limited since definitions of what qualifies as international terrorism are influenced by U.S. policy preferences at a given time. For further discussion of this problem, see Falkenrath (2000). For an early review of the purposes and methodologies of a variety of terrorism databases, see Fowler (1981).

36. For a discussion of how intractable conflicts widen through "spillover," see Sandole (1999, pp. 143–150).

CHAPTER 2

1. See Schelling (1966, p. 2).
2. See Morgan (1977, p. 17).
3. See Harkabi (1990, 221), quoted in Almog (2004, p. 7).
4. See Zeev (1990, p. 65), quoted in Almog (2004, p. 7). For more discussion and background on the theory of deterrence, see Schelling (1963), George and Smoke (1974), Harvey (1977), Jervis (1979), and Pape (1996).
5. The task force included 25 people from each branch of the military and from various governmental agencies. See National War College (2002).
6. Quoted from Doron Almog (2004, p. 15).
7. See The White House (February 2003), p. 15. See also U.S. Department of Defense, *Transformation Planning Guidance,* Washington: GPO, April 2003, retrieved from http://www.defenselink.mil/brac/docs/transformationplanningapr03.pdf, and Prepared Testimony on the FY 2003 Defense Budget Request to the SAC-D, testimony of U.S. Deputy Secretary of Defense Paul Wolfowitz before the U.S. Senate Appropriations Committee, Subcommittee on Defense, February 27, 2002, retrieved from http://www.defenselink.mil/speeches/2002/s20020227-depsecdef.html
8. See Bush (2003, pp. 2–3).
9. See Bush (2002b, p. 15). Note: The distinction between preventative and preemptive war is a fine one. Dan Reiter describes it as follows: "Preventive war occurs when one state perceives the balance of power shifting against it and attacks sooner rather than later, when conditions would be less favorable. Preemptive war occurs when one state attacks in order to forestall a perceived imminent attack" (Reiter, 2003, p. 33).
10. See Bush (2002a).
11. See Cheney (2002).
12. Department of Defense News Transcript, August 19, 2002. Retrieved from http://www.dod.gov/transcripts/2002/t09122002_t0819foxanew.html
13. CNN Television. (2002, September 8). *Search for the smoking gun.* Interview of Condoleezza Rice by Wolf Blitzer.
14. See McLemee (2002).
15. See Schroeder (2002). See also Franklin (2004). And for an earlier discussion of the morality of preemption see Roberts (1998).
16. See Peters (2003).
17. See Brinsfield (2003). Similar conclusions were reached by Michael Walzer (2003), known for his classic work on just and unjust wars (Walzer, 2000).
18. See CNN Inside Politics (2002). See also Scowcroft (2002).
19. See Jervis (2003). See also Mearsheimer and Walt (2003).

20. Quoted in Panel Discussion, The Fletcher School, Tufts University (2004).
21. See Gaddis (2002, p. 50). See also Gaddis (2004, pp. 7–33).
22. See Hartung (2003).
23. See Cordesman (2004).
24. Although these sums are high, some observers pointed out that by historical standards the war was not necessarily a huge burden for the United States. For example, Peter Grier observed that, "even if war funding is included, the Defense budget would be some 4 percent of gross domestic product—compared to the 6 percent or so it reached during the Reagan years" (Grier, 2004).
25. See Weisman (2005).
26. See Associated Press (2005).
27. See Iraqi Body Count. Retrieved from http://www.iraqbodycount.net/
28. See Roberts, Lafta, Garfield, Khudhairi, and Burnham (2004).
29. See Conetta (2003).
30. Sanger (2003).
31. See Pincus and Priest (2003).
32. See International Institute for Strategic Studies (2003).
33. See Center for Strategic and International Studies (CSIS) (2003a, 2003b).
34. See Center for Strategic and International Studies (CSIS) (2004a). Evidence of new links and webs of relationships between local "self-proclaimed Islamic terrorist groups" and al Qaeda was also emerging in Southeast Asia. See Ministry of Home Affairs, Republic of Singapore (2003).
35. See Center for Strategic and International Studies (CSIS) (2004a).
36. See BBC News (2003).
37. See Krane (2004). See also Center for Strategic and International Studies (CSIS) (2004c).
38. Center for Strategic and International Studies (CSIS) (2004d). According to a new IISS report authored by Chipman (2004), the Iraq war had boosted al-Qaeda recruitment and it remained a "viable network of networks." For more on the rejuvenated, decentralized, and networked al-Qaeda, see Gunaratna (2004). See also Pillar (2004).
39. See Obaid and Cordesman (2005).
40. Cited in McCarthy (2004).
41. Center for Strategic and International Studies (CSIS) (2004b).
42. As early as 1993, Harvard's Samuel P. Huntington put forth the theory that world politics was entering "a new phase." In this phase, "the fundamental source of conflict" would not be primarily ideological or economic but cultural. Huntington believed that in the absence of a more profound understanding of the basic philosophical assumptions underlying other civilizations and how they see their interests, there would be an increasing tendency for people all

over the world to define their identity in ethnic and religious terms and that this tendency would lead to a growing adoption of "us" versus "them" worldviews. In this environment, what he called the "fault lines between civilizations" were likely to become the battle lines of the future" (Huntington, 1993). See also Sandole (2005).

43. See Singer (2004, pp. 141–142).
44. See Singer (2004).
45. See Pew Research Center for the People and the Press (2003).
46. See Pew Research Center for the People and the Press (2004).
47. See Singer (2004, p. 141).
48. See Rumsfeld (2003). The ability of the U.S. to sustain the war in Iraq was also a growing concern for the Congressional Budget Office. See U.S. Congressional Budget Office (2003).
49. See Krueger and Laitin (2004).
50. See Record (2003).
51. See Record (2003, p. 4), citing Hoffman (2003, p. 22).
52. See Record (2003, p. 4), citing Byman (2003). Also, see Arquilla, Ronfeldt, and Zanini (2002).
53. See Record (2003, p. 4).
54. See Rice (2005).
55. See Rice (2005).
56. See Glaser (2005c).
57. See Glaser (2005b).
58. See Glaser (2005a).

CHAPTER 3

1. On problems defining terrorism, see Malik (2001).
2. See Tilly (2004, p. 5).
3. See Tilly (2004).
4. See Schmid and Jongman (1988, pp. 5–6).
5. See Laqueur (1999, p. 6).
6. See Adcock and Collier (2001).
7. See Marshall (2002, p. 2).
8. See Laqueur (1987, p. 72).
9. See Carr (2002, pp. 6–7).
10. See Hoffman (1998, p. 43).
11. See Schmid and Jongman (1998).
12. See Hoffman (1998, p. 31).
13. See Marshall (2002, p. 3).

14. See Cunningham (2002, p. 5).
15. See McCauley (1991).
16. See Hoffman (1998, p. 31).
17. See Sandole (2002, p. 89).
18. See Falkenrath (2000, p. 10).
19. See Brian (2002), quoted in Kegley (1990, p. 29).
20. See Crenshaw (1981) in Schmid and Jongman (1998, p. 35).
21. See Jenkins (2002), quoted in Kegley (1990, p. 28). See also Oots (1986, p. 81).
22. See Enders and Sandler (2002, pp. 145–146).
23. See Enders and Sandler (2002). See also Hoffman (1998).
24. Quoted in Hoffman (1998, p. 38).
25. Quoted in Hoffman (1998, p. 38).
26. See Cunningham (2002) for a thorough review.
27. Rosendorff and Sandler (2004, p. 658), for example, distinguish between "spectacular" attacks such as September 11 and the March 2004 Madrid train bombings and lower-level attacks.
28. See Wilkinson (1986, p. 182).
29. See National Foreign Assessment Center, Central Intelligence Agency (1978, p. 1).
30. See Enders and Sandler (2002, p. 148).
31. Dekmeijian describes politicized Islam as an "ideology of protest against ruling elites who are charged with deviating from the true faith." As such, he argues that it is an "ideology of opposition against those in power" (Dekmejian, 1985, p. 176).
32. See Baylouney (2004). See also Wiktorowicz (2004).
33. See Clausewitz (1976, p. 88).
34. See Record (2003).
35. Remarks by President Bush at the 2002 Graduation Exercise of the United States Military Academy at West Point. Retrieved from http://www.whitehouse.gov/news/releases/ 2002/06/20020601-3.html
36. See Rumsfeld (2001).
37. See Record (2003, pp. 2–3).
38. On July 18, 2005, in an address to the National Press Club, General Richard B. Myers, chairman of the Joint Chiefs of Staff, said that he had "objected to the use of the term 'war on terrorism' for some time because if you call it a war, then you think of people in uniform as being the solution." Others in the administration were beginning to use new terms such as *struggle* or *struggle against extremism*. In mid-July, in a speech in Annapolis, Secretary of Defense Donald Rumsfeld, for example, described America's efforts in terms of a "global struggle against the enemies of freedom, the enemies of civilization." Around the

same time, Steven Hadley, national security advisor, opined that America's cause was broader than a war: "It's a global struggle against extremism" (Schmitt & Shanker, 2005). See also Holmes (2005).

39. See Stevenson (2005).

CHAPTER 4

1. See Popper (1972).
2. See Gurr (1970).
3. See Senechal de la Roche (1996). See also Senechal de la Roche (2004, p. 2).
4. See, for example, Kepel (1993, p. 20). Kepel stresses the feelings of powerlessness and highlights the "loss of reference points" and "loss of identity" that occurred in Egypt. See also Haddad (1992).
5. See Wiktorowicz (2004, p. 7). Economic explanations for Islamist activism were put forward early on by Ibrahim (1980). His research, cited in Wiktorowicz, showed that individuals with high levels of education, who migrated to urban centers in search of employment, often felt cut off from their roots and blocked from social mobility, suffered a sense of "social alienation and anomie," and became increasingly "vulnerable to the Islamist message of tradition." Similar arguments are made by Ayubi (1991, pp. 159–160). Ayubi found that backing for Islamic and Islamist causes was directly related to growing frustrations arising from thwarted economic expectations. Countering the findings of Krueger and Maleckova (2002) and of Berrebi (2003), Saleh (2004) also stresses the importance of economic determinants in violent attacks by Palestinians on Israelis. Others have stressed the importance of cultural imperialism in the production of Islamic activism. See, in particular, Burgat (1993). Still others have highlighted the importance of authoritarian rule at home. For example, Esposito (1995, p. 15) argues that alienation arising from an unresponsive government and lack of political participation have played important causal roles in Islamist activism. See also McGlinchey (2004) who attributes higher levels of militant Islam in Central Asia to differences in levels of authoritarian rule.
6. See Dekmejian (1995, p. 6). See also Tibi (1998) and Lewis (2003). See also Sprinzak (1991), who claims that terrorism is often the end result of a process of delegitimization.
7. See Crenshaw (1981).
8. For a fuller discussion of this issue, see Rubenstein (2003).
9. See Pape (2003, p. 344).
10. See Enders and Sandler (1993, p. 830).
11. See Sandler and Enders (2004, p. 311).

12. See Sandler and Enders (2004). See also Enders and Sandler (2004).

13. See Sandler, Tschirhart, and Cauley (1983). See also Enders and Sandler (2004). For more on how those who engage in terrorism may select their targets, see Sandler and Lapan (1988).

14. See Duffield (2002). See also Iannaccone (2003).

15. There is good empirical evidence that terrorist middlemen often have interests and preferences that are not aligned with their leadership. See Shapiro and Siegel (2005).

16. See, for example, Lake (2002, pp. 15–29); see also Van Dyke and Soule (2002).

17. See McAdam (1982).

18. See, for example, Gamson (1975), Tilly (1978), and McCarthy and Zald (1977).

19. See McAdam (1982).

20. On the importance of the mosque, see Parsa (1989); see also Wickham (1977, 2002).

21. See Esposito and Voll (1996); see also Langhor (2001).

22. See Wiktorowicz (2001, 2004); Robinson (2003, 2004); Munson (2001) and Hafez (2004).

23. See Frey (2004, p. 510).

24. Laqueur (1977, p. 106) has argued that media attention is often the primary goal.

25. There is good evidence that terrorist acts can have a destabilizing effect, for example, by reducing tourism and foreign direct investment. See Fleischer and Buccola (2002), Enders et al. (1992), and Enders and Sandler (1996). There is also good evidence that terrorism has negative impacts on gross domestic income and trade. See Abadie and Gardeazabal (2003) and Nitsch and Schumacher (2004).

26. See Crenshaw (1981, pp. 385–395).

27. See Enders and Sandler (1993, p. 830); see also Enders and Sandler (2004).

28. Lake (2002, p. 16) argues that "a disproportionate response" is frequently what terrorists want to provoke and tactical innovation, as McAdam (1983) observed can often quicken the pace of insurgent movements.

29. See Tovar (1986); see also Wilkinson (1986).

30. See Bueno de Mesquita (2005, p. 516).

31. See Malvesti (2001). Malvesti observes that over a 16-year period from 1983 to 1998, the United States applied military force in response to only three international terrorist events: the 1986 Libyan bombing of a West German discotheque, the 1993 Iraqi assassination attempt on former President Bush in Kuwait, and the 1998 bombings of U.S. embassies in East Africa by bin Laden operatives.

32. See Tilly (1978).

33. For a full discussion, see Lichbach (1987).

34. See Lichbach (1987).

35. See Rosendorff and Sandler (2004, p. 657).
36. See Rosendorff and Sandler (2005, p. 176).
37. See Brophy-Baermann and Conybeare (1994).
38. See Enders and Sandler (1993, p. 835).
39. See Bloom (2004).
40. See Martinez-Herrara (2003).
41. See Woods (2003).
42. See Hafez and Wiktorowicz (2004).
43. See McGlinchey (2004).
44. See Wiktorowicz (2001).
45. See Goldstone and Tilly (2001, p. 181).
46. See Lichbach (1987, p. 270).
47. See Hafez and Wikotorowicz (2004, p. 70). See also Mason and Krane (1989) who show that escalating state-sanctioned terror in the form of death squads in El Salvador had the effect of increasing rather than decreasing opposition. Of interest is their additional finding that escalating repression may continue not because it is expected to succeed but because the weakness of a state makes it difficult to pursue more accommodative programs.
48. See Gurr and Goldstone (1991).
49. See Horne (1977).
50. See Deutsch (1973).
51. See Pruitt and Rubin (1986, p. 64).
52. See Pruitt and Rubin (1986, p. 74). See also Opotow (2000, p. 411) and Kriesberg (1998, p. 169).
53. See Sandole (1998).
54. See Karklins and Peterson (1989).
55. See Lohmann (1994).
56. See Francisco (2001). For how "self-stimulating/self-perpetuating conflict processes" can be generated under such circumstances, see Sandole (1999, p. 80).
57. See Mack (1975) for his analysis of the importance of resolve in asymmetric conflicts. Arreguin-Toft (2001, p. 94) argues that resolve and interest, as in "balance of resolve" and "balance of interest," although analytically distinct, move in the same direction and are, therefore, interchangeable.
58. See Arreguin-Toft (2001, p. 99).
59. See Arreguin-Toft (2001, p. 108).
60. See Arreguin-Toft (2001, pp. 100–104).
61. See Mao (1966, p. 72). For further descriptions of insurgent and terror tactics in asymmetric conflicts see Mao (1961), Taber (1965), Marighella (1985), and Betts (2002).
62. See Arreguin-Toft (2001, p. 101).

63. See Kiras (2002). See also Callwell (1996, p. 21). For a discussion of the distinctions between and overlap of terrorism, guerilla war, and insurgency, see Merari (1993). For a longer explanation of insurgency, small war, or asymmetric conflict, see Cassidy (2000).
64. See Sandler (2003, p. 780).
65. Studies by Enders and Sandler have shown that in response to government initiatives, terrorists often shift into new modes of attack (Enders & Sandler, 1993).
66. See Enders and Sandler (1990, 1993).
67. See Enders and Sandler (2005).
68. See Rumsfeld (2005).

CHAPTER 5

1. See Enders and Sandler (2004).
2. See Enders and Sandler (2005, p. 259).
3. See Box and Tiao (1975).
4. See Druckman (2005, Section 3.3).
5. See Druckman (2005).
6. See StatSoft Electronic Textbook (1984–2003).
7. See Wichern and Jones (1977).
8. See Pankratz (1991, p. 263).
9. See Yin and Newman (1999).
10. See Mooradian and Druckman (1999).
11. See Brophy-Baermann and Conybeare (1994).
12. See Enders and Sandler (1990).
13. See Nelson and Scot (1992). See also Scott (2001).
14. See Enders and Sandler (1993).
15. See SAS/ETS Users Guide (1999). See also McDowall, McCleary, Meidinger, and Hay (1980).
16. See Shambaugh and Josiger (2004).
17. There is no precise method of listing populations by religious denomination. However, estimates based on samples have been made. To extract incidents in Muslim populations of 50% or more, I used a Wikipedia table available at http://en.wikipedia.org/wiki/Islam_by_country. This table of countries by percentage Muslim population was built using the U.S. State Department's International Religious Freedom Report 2004, as well as the CIA Factbook and adherents.com. See Appendix B.
18. See chapter 6, "Bird's-Eye View" for methodology for extracting attacks by Islamist and Islamist national separatist groups. See Appendix C for a listing of these groups.

19. See Enders and Sandler (2005).
20. See Cook and Campbell (1979).
21. See Enders and Sandler (2005, p. 260).
22. See Druckman (2005, Section 11.4).
23. See Stern (2003, p. 268).
24. See Public Broadcasting Service Frontline.
25. See Stern (2003, p. 192).
26. SOURCES: *International Terrorism: Attributes of International Events* (ITER-ATE, Mickolus, 2003, 1968–2003; Rand–St. Andrews Chronology of International Terrorism (RAND–MIPT), provided by the Oklahoma City Memorial Institute for the Prevention of Terrorism (MIPT), www.mipt.org (counts calculated from Web information); U.S. Department of State, Patterns of Global Terrorism (1968–2003).
27. See, for example, Cauley and Im (1988), Brophy-Baermann and Conybeare (1994), Enders and Sandler (1990, 1992, 1993, 1996, 2000, 2002, 2004, 2005); Enders, Sandler, and Cauley (1990), Enders, Sandler, and Parise (1992); O'Brien (1996), Lai (2003, 2004), and Shambaugh and Josiger (2004).
28. Key sources include the Associated Press, United Press International, Reuters tickers, the Foreign Broadcast Information Service, the world press, and major television and radio news networks.
29. See Mickolus, Sandler, Murdoch, and Fleming (2003, p. 2).
30. See Mickolus et al. (2003).
31. See MIPT (2002).
32. See MIPT (2002).
33. I defined duplicates as descriptions of the same incidents occurring on the same day in the same location. Further discussion of duplicates is offered in chapter 6.
34. ANOVA (analysis of variance), the independent t-test (also called unpaired t-test or two-sample t-test), and chi-square are statistical measures that can be used to test for differences across independent samples or groups. ANOVA tests the null hypothesis that two or more means from independent groups are equal. The independent t-test tests the null hypothesis that two means from independent groups are equal. The chi-square test, which is used for frequency data, tests the null hypothesis that proportions from two or more independent groups are equal.
35. JMP is a statistical analysis software program developed by SAS for personal computers. It is widely used in universities for teaching statistics.
36. See Albritton (1981).
37. See Cook and Campbell (1979, p. 234).
38. See Cook and Campbell (1979, pp. 207–232).

39. See Midlarsky, Crenshaw, and Yohida (1980), Brophy-Baermann and Conybeare (1994), Enders and Sandler (1993), O'Brien (1996), Weimann and Brosius (1988), and Willer (2004).
40. See Rock (1995, p. 210).
41. See Rock (1995).
42. Eviews is a sophisticated data analysis program that is particularly suited for studies involving regression analysis with time series data. It was originally developed by economists in the Time Series Processor software for large computers and is often used in econometrics and forecasting.
43. The term *white noise process* is used to refer to a time series in which the observed *variance* (i.e., the noise signal) has no autocorrelation (i.e., the variance of one variable is not dependent on the variance of previous variables). The signal (i.e., change or trend in a variable) is thus white in the spatial frequency domain. Log transformation of a time series may be required to achieve a white noise process before regression can be performed.
44. See Manning (1998).
45. The residuals should be white noise or independent when their distributions are normal.
46. See Neter, Wasserman, and Whitmore (1988).
47. The Durbin–Watson test is the standard test for autocorrelation. It tests the time series assumption that error terms are uncorrelated. The value of "*d*" ranges from 0 to 4. Values close to 0 indicate extreme positive autocorrelation, values close to 4 indicate extreme negative autocorrelation, and values close to 2 indicate no serial autocorrelation. As a rule of thumb, "*d*" should be between 1.5 and 2.5 to indicate independence of observations.
48. See individual tables in Appendix D.
49. Eviews 4.1 manual.
50. Eviews 4.1 manual.
51. For example, the dummy variable for the GWOT was coded as "0" for the first 35 quarterly intervals (through the third quarter of 2001) and "1" for the next 13 quarterly intervals (through the last quarter of 2004). In contrast, the dummy variable for the release of photos from Abu Ghraib was coded as "0" for the first 45 intervals (through the first quarter of 2004) and as "1" thereafter.
52. The term *predictor* variable is often used interchangeably with the term *independent variable* to describe the intervention in time series intervention analyses that use regression. However, as noted earlier, there is a body of opinion to the effect that the terms *independent variable* and *dependent variable* should be reserved for experimental studies. I use the terms in the text to avoid confusion since they are used in the regression output provided in the regression output tables (Appendix D).

53. See Cook and Campbell (1979). See also Stern and Druckman (2000).
54. See Mickolus (2002, p. 153).
55. In the latter case, hundreds or even thousands of events may need to be recoded. See Koopman and Rucht (2002, p. 239).
56. See Koopman and Rucht (2002).
57. Personal communication with James "Chip" O. Ellis, Research and Program Coordinator, Memorial Institute for the Prevention of Terrorism, by e-mail 11/11/05.
58. The ITERATE Coding Book is available from Edward Mickolus at Vinyard Software in Dunn Loring, Virginia. Since ITERATE data for 2004 was only available in text form, I also used the Coding Book to code ITERATE incidents for 2004.
59. See Robson (2002, p. 100).
60. See Robson (2002), who describes external validity in terms of generalizability.
61. See Stern and Druckman (2000, p. 51).
62. See George and Bennett (2005).
63. Recent simulation work, for example, has extended our knowledge about how the GWOT has affected terrorist financing (see Kiser, 2004).
64. See Stern and Druckman (2000, p. 71).
65. See Cook and Campbell (1979, p. 225).
66. Personal communication, Michael Eaddy, Ph.D., statistician, March 2005.
67. See Campbell and Fiske (1959).
68. See Stern and Druckman (2000, p. 82).

CHAPTER 6

1. Quotation from "The Messiness of History," Peter Viereck's final lecture at Holyoke College in 1997. See Reiss (2005).
2. In a separate more fine-tuned analysis, using the 13 UN Macro Region categories, North Africa (collapsed into the Middle East and North Africa) contributed only 5% of the total and West Asia contributed 28%. The distribution in Europe was as follows: Western Europe 11%, Southern Europe 9%, Northern Europe 4%, and Eastern Europe 2%. In Sub-Saharan Africa, West Africa was found to contribute 2%, East Africa 5%, and Southern and Middle Africa 2%. East and Southeast Asia still contributed 7% in combination. South and Central America contributed a combination of 13%.
3. In rare instances (example provided of multiple bombings reported by ITERATE in Colombia in 1999), when the month of an event but not the day was reported, I divided the sum of events for the month by the number of days. This procedure may have inflated the number of days for that month and quarter, but

since it occurred only once or twice it is unlikely to have had a major effect on the results.

4. For simplicity and to standardize the two databases, I collapsed disputed territories such as Kashmir and Chechnya (ITERATE) and the Occupied Territories (treated separately in RAND but not in ITERATE) into their official countries of record (e.g., Kashmir into India, Chechnya into Russia, and the Occupied Territories into Israel). However, since both databases treated Northern Ireland as a separate territory, I left that territory intact.

5. To better capture suicide attacks, I made an exception for suicide bombings when ITERATE's textual description, but not its classification, referred to a suicide bombing and RAND's classification was one of suicide bombing. As will be discussed later in this chapter, I collapsed hostage events, including kidnappings, skyjackings, and barricade hostage seizures, for the time series analyses. I also collapsed explosive bombings and fire bombings for these analyses.

6. ITERATE provided a code for incidents for which deaths or injuries were believed to have occurred although the number of deaths or injuries was not known at the time of entry into its database. RAND almost always listed a number based on a cited news report for deaths and injuries. In rare cases, where it used the category "unknown," it was possible to determine from the text description if the incident was associated with deaths or injuries.

7. Each of the databases reported a number for injuries. I classified incidents as associated with injuries if an injury was reported for the incident in either database.

8. I used ITERATE's classification for this measure. I used RAND's textual description, where necessary, to code to ITERATE.

9. See Appendix C for a listing of perpetrator groups I assigned to this category.

10. In a small number of cases, one but not the other database coded the perpetrator as "unknown." In these cases, I assumed that the database that coded the perpetrator group by name had more information. As a result, I used the known perpetrator name for classification. Also, in a small number of cases, one database gave a general category (e.g., Indeterminate Arab in ITERATE). If the other database supplied a named group, I used the named group for classification. Where the two databases differed on the name of a particular group for an incident, I standardized to ITERATE. These differences had no impact on the classification since the type of perpetrator group always fell into the same category.

11. See Appendix A for the variables used in the time series analyses. See Appendix D for the tables produced by the time series analyses for this variable and other variables in the analysis.

12. The F-statistic is a test of the hypothesis that all the coefficients in a regression are zero (except the intercept or constant). If the F-statistic exceeds a critical level, at least one of the coefficients is probably nonzero. This probability is reflected in the p-value. In the time series analyses shown here, one can tell at a glance if one should reject or accept the hypothesis that all the coefficients are zero. Normally, a probability that is lower than .05 is taken as strong evidence of rejection of the null hypothesis. As shown in the tables in Appendix D, the t-statistic was used to test the hypothesis that a particular coefficient was zero. In this section, I provide the p-value for each coefficient in the regression. For clarity, I express each coefficient in terms of percentage change. Thus, a coefficient of .50 is expressed as a 50% increase and a coefficient of –.50 is expressed as a 50% decrease. As shown in Appendix D, coefficients, t-statistics and p-values were produced for time and for each of the four independent (predictor) variables.

13. It is possible that exclusion of incidents in Israel and the Occupied Territories would have changed these results (decreasing the impact of the GWOT and increasing the impact of the War in Iraq—as outlined previously). This analysis was not performed.

14. See Appendix B for a listing of the 41 countries meeting the criterion of having 50% or greater Muslim populations.

15. See Enders and Sandler (2005).

16. It was not possible to log transform this variable. The regression was, therefore, performed without log transformation, and raw numbers rather than coefficients for percentage increase are provided here.

17. See Hoffman (1998).

18. Confidence in statistical significance is often enhanced when there is also convergence or triangulation of results.

19. Increases in the frequency of terrorist incidents may be associated with decreases in intensity (lethality) and vice versa. One of the reasons I have included multiple measures in the analysis of all incidents and more than one measure in this subanalysis is because any one measure, taken alone, could give an incomplete picture.

CHAPTER 7

1. For a fuller discussion of the difficulties associated with extrapolating such findings, see Sandole (1999, chaps. 4 and 5).

2. See Zakaria (2005).

3. Others have argued that defensive moves by some governments make other governments more vulnerable since in this situation terrorists tend to displace attacks to countries that are less well protected (see Arce & Sandler, 2005).

4. See Enders and Sandler (2005, p. 259).

5. See Cunningham (2002, p. 5). There is also a need for taxonomies that incorporate the causes of different types of terrorism and the conditions under which acts of terrorism (and counterterrorism) occur. See also Sandole (2002) for preliminary work relating to terrorism in this area.

6. The RAND–MIPT database is an exception. This database has been keeping track of domestic incidents in text format, but only since 1998.

7. Previous work has shown that media reports tend to be less inclusive than police archives when it comes to covering "protest" events. See Peter Hocke (1999). Police archives could be used to better capture domestic terrorist incidents.

8. Doug (Sgt) Sample. *Fallujah secure, but not yet safe, marine commander says.* U.S. Department of Defense American Forces Information Service News Articles, Washington, DC, November 18, 2004. Retrieved from http://www. defenselink.mil/news/Nov2004/n11182004_2004111803.html

9. For recent work in this area, see Pape (2005) and Bloom (2005).

10. Reciprocity and responsiveness research, developed in the context of the negotiation of international conflicts, could be extended to terrorism-counterterrorism clashes. See, for example, Patchen (1987,1998b), Parks and Komorita (1998), and Druckman (1998). Coding methods for studying sequences of social movement interactions (e.g., movement–countermovement, movement–bystander), developed in the context of the study of protest, could also be extended to the topic. See, for example, McPhail and Schweingruber (1999).

11. Because there is "no single best way to develop knowledge," Stern and Druckman (2000, p. 82) observe that the use of multiple methods, as well as multiple sources of data, perspectives, and modes of analysis, can "act as partial correctives for the limitations of research approaches that rely on different ones."

12. See Yin (1989).

13. See Druckman (2005, chap. 7).

14. For examples of classic work using process tracing, see Faure (1994) and Putnam (1993). For more recent work related to terrorism, see Charters and Walker (2002/2003).

15. Recent simulation work, for example, has contributed to a better understanding of how the GWOT has affected terrorist financing (see Kiser, 2004).

16. See Crenshaw (1991).

17. See McCauley (1991, p. 134).

18. See Sprinzak (1991, p. 56). See also Druckman and Green (1986). These authors discuss the important role of "legitimacy" in political instability in the Philippines.

19. Bin Laden's articulated goal of driving out "foreign troops" is not atypical according to Pape (2005), who shows that suicide terrorism is largely a response

to foreign occupation and gives as many as 400 examples from Lebanon to Chechnya.

20. See Gunaratna (2002, p. 298). For further discussion of religion and sacred values as motivating or rallying factors for terrorism, see Juergensmeyer (2003). See also Stern (2003).

21. See Huntington (1993, p. 22).

22. The White House (2005).

23. See De Wijk (2002, p. 86).

24. In June 2005, Hezbollah swept the elections in southern Lebanon and Hamas began to make inroads on the traditional Fatah party in Palestine. In Egypt, the government became so concerned about the rising support of the Islamist organization, the Muslim Brotherhood, that it excluded it from upcoming elections (Syed, 2005). More recently, in January 2006, Hamas scored an overwhelming victory in Palestinian elections, taking 76 out of 132 seats, and deposing the ruling Fatah party who won only 43 seats (Erlanger, 2006).

25. See Al-Sayyid (2003).

26. See Nye (2001) and Nye (2004, pp. 7–8).

27. See Nye (2004).

28. See Jenkins (2002).

29. See Posen (2001/2002).

30. See Cronin (2002). See also Cortright, Millar, Lopez, and Gerber (2003) on the importance of a global cooperative approach.

31. See Machiavelli (1988, p. 59).

32. See Patchen (1998a, p. 261). See also George and Smoke (1974, p. 33) and Fisher (1969, p. 106).

33. See Cortright (2000).

34. See Gorman, Robinson, and Walsh (2005).

35. See Cortright (2000).

36. See Druckman (1986) and Druckman, Husbands, and Johnson (1991).

37. Although some take the view that Islamist political participation cannot be reconciled with secular democracy, the evidence from a recent book on the successes of democratic federalism in Nigeria, where Islamist Sharia law and secular law coexist, suggests that this is not the case (Paden, 2005).

38. See McNamara (1995).

39. It is likely that offense was also taken when, soon after September 11, Israeli Prime Minister Ariel Sharon declared, "This is a turning point in the international war on terrorism. This is a war between good and evil. The fight of the free world against the forces of darkness" (see *Washington Times*, 2001). Similarly, it was not well received when Italian Prime Minister, Silvio Berlusconi, made remarks to the effect that Western civilization was superior to that of the Islamic world

and urged Europe to "reconstitute itself on the basis of its Christian roots." See Erlanger (2001, September 27).

40. See Atran (2004, p. 86).
41. See Posen (2001/2002, p. 51).
42. Previous quantitative work has shown that countries with fewer civil liberties are more likely to be "wellsprings" of international terrorism than countries with greater civil liberties (see Krueger & Maleckova, 2003a, p. B10). There is also good evidence in the qualitative literature to support the contention that terrorism mounted by militant Islamist terrorist groups is more likely to occur under more repressive regimes (see, e.g., McGlinchey, 2004). An important result of his in-depth case study of militant Islamic movements in post-Soviet Central Asia was the finding that calls for violent opposition had greater "resonance in totalitarian regimes than in authoritarian states that, even to a limited extent, allow some contestation."
43. See Paden and Singer (2003, pp. 13–14).
44. Quoted in Prestowitz (2003, p. 275).
45. See Peters (2004).

APPENDICES

1. The relatively low R-square in Table 1 and other tables shown here is a function of the log transformation of the dependent variable of interest (in this case, number of incidents). The original R-square (before transformation) was very high. Low R-squares are considered very respectable in time series analyses of log transformed variables.
2. For log transformed variables, the coefficient is represented by a fraction (e.g., 0.74). This fraction can be interpreted as a percentage change. For untransformed variables (all of the percentage variables), the coefficient can also be interpreted as a percentage change. For Number of Hostage Takings, which could not be transformed, the coefficient indicates the actual average number of increase.
3. The individual cell chi-squares indicated that the largest contributions to the overall chi-square came from the Middle East and North African region, Sub-Saharan Africa, and the East Asia/Pacific region.
4. The individual cell chi-squares indicated that the largest contributions to the overall chi-square came from the categories business, foreign military, host government military, and type of immediate victim classified as unknown.

BIBLIOGRAPHY

Abadie, A., & Gardeazabal, J. (2003). The economic costs of conflict: A case study for the Basque country. *American Economic Review, 93*, 113–132.

Adcock, R., & Collier, D. (2001). Measurement validity: A shared standard for qualitative and quantitative research. *American Political Science Review, 95*(3), 529–546.

Albritton, R. B. (1981). A comparison of Box-Jenkins-Tiao and multivariate least squares techniques for intervention analysis. *Political Methodology, 7*, 13–29.

Almog, D. (2004). Cumulative deterrence and the war on terrorism. *Parameters, 34*(4), 4–19.

Al-Sayyid, M. K. (2003, January). *The other face of the Islamist movement.* Global Policy Program Working Paper No. 33. Carnegie Endowment for International Peace, Democracy and Rule of Law Project.

Arce, D., & Sandler, T. (2005). A game-theoretic analysis. *Journal of Conflict Resolution, 49*(2), 193–200.

Arquilla, J., Ronfeldt, D., & Zanin, M. (2002). Networks, netwar, and information-age terrorism. In D. H. Russell & R. L. Sawyer (Eds.), *Terrorism and counter-terrorism: Understanding the new security environment, readings and interpretations* (pp. 96–119). New York: McGraw-Hill.

Arreguin-Toft, I. (2001). How the weak win wars. *International Security, 26*(1), 93–128.

Asprey, R. B. (1994). *War in the shadows: The classic history of guerilla warfare from ancient Persia to the present.* New York: Little, Brown.

Associated Press. (2005, January 16). A daily look at U.S. Iraq military deaths.

Atran, S. (2004). Mishandling suicide terrorism. *Washington Quarterly, 27*(3), 67–90.

Ayubi, N. (1991). *Political Islam religion and politics.* London: Routledge.

Baylouny, A. M. (2004). Emotions, poverty or politics: Misconceptions about Islamic movements. *Strategic Insights, 3*(1). Center for Contemporary Conflict. Retrieved from http://www.ccc.nps.navy.mil/si/2004/jan/baylounyJan04.asp

BBC News. (2003, May 13). Chechnya death toll rises. Retrieved from http://news.bbc.co.uk/1/hi/world/europe/3022379.stm

Berrebi, C. (2003). *Evidence about the link between education, poverty and terrorism among Palestinians.* Princeton University Industrial Relations Working Paper No. 477. Retrieved from http://www.irs.princeton.edu/pubs/working_papers.html

Betts, R. K. (2002). The soft underbelly of American primacy: Tactical advantages of terror. *Political Science Quarterly, 117*(1), 19–36.

Bloom, M. (2004). Palestinian suicide bombing: Public support, market share and outbidding. *Political Science Quarterly, 119*(1), 61–88.

Bloom, M. (2005). *Dying to kill: The allure of suicide terrorism.* New York: Columbia University Press.

Box, G. E. P., & Jenkins, G. M. (1976). *Time series analysis.* San Francisco: Holden-Day.

Box, G. E. P., & Tiao, G. C. (1975). Intervention analysis with applications to economic and environmental problems. *Journal of the American Statistical Association, 70*, 70–79.

Brinsfield, J. (2003, March 30). Going against rules no reason to rejoice. *Atlanta Journal-Constitution*, p. C2.

Brophy-Baermann, B., & Conybeare, J. A. C. (1994). Retaliating against terrorism: Rational expectations and the optimality of rules versus discretion. *American Journal of Political Science, 38*(1), 196–210.

Bueno de Mesquita, E. (2005). The quality of terror. *American Journal of Political Science, 49*(3), 515–530.

Burgat, F. (1993). *The Islamic movement in North Africa* (W. Dowell, trans.). Austin: Center for Middle Eastern Studies, University of Texas.

Bush, G. W. (2001, September 20). *Presidential address to a Joint Session of Congress and the American People.* Washington, DC.

Bush, G. W. (2002a, June 1). *Graduation speech at West Point.* Retrieved from http://www.nti.org/e_research/official_docs/pres/bush_wp_prestrike.pdf

Bush, G. W. (2002b, September). *The national security strategy of the United States of America.* Washington, DC: The White House. Retrieved from http://www.whitehouse.gov/nsc/nss.html

Bush, G. W. (2003, February). *The national strategy for combating terrorism.* Washington, DC: The White House.

Byman, D. (2003). Scoring the war on terrorism. *National Interest, Summer*, 79–80.

Callwell, C. E. (1996). *Small wars: Their principles and practice* (3rd ed.). Lincoln: University of Nebraska Press.

Campbell, D. T. & Fiske, D. W. (1959). Convergent and discriminant validation by the multitrait-multimethod matrix. *Psychological Bulletin, 56*, 81–105.

Carr, C. (2002). *The lesson of terror: A history of warfare against civilians, why it has always failed and why it will fail again.* New York: Random House.

Cassidy, R. (2000). Why great powers fight small wars badly. *Military Review, September/October*, 41–53.

Cauley, J., & Im, E. (1988). Intervention policy analysis of skyjackings and other terrorist incidents. The American Economic Review, 78, No. 2:27–31.

Center for Strategic and International Studies (CSIS). (2003a, August). *Transnational threats update 1*, No. 11. Retrieved from http://www.csis.org/TNT/ttu/ttu_0308.pdf

Center for Strategic and International Studies (CSIS). (2003b, October). *Transnational threats update 2*, No. 1. Retrieved from http://www.csis.org/tnt/ttu/ttu_0310.pdf

Center for Strategic and International Studies (CSIS). (2004a, March). *Transnational threats update 2*, No. 6. Retrieved from http://www.csis.org/TNT/ttu/ttu_0403.pdf

Center for Strategic and International Studies (CSIS). (2004b, July). *Transnational threats update 2*, No. 10. Retrieved from http://www.csis.org/media/csis/pubs/ttu_0407.pdf

Center for Strategic and International Studies (CSIS). (2004c, May). *Transnational threats update 2*, No. 8. Retrieved from http://www.csis.org/media/csis/pubs/ttu_0405.pdf

Center for Strategic and International Studies (CSIS). (2004d, June). *Transnational threats update 2*, No. 9. Retrieved from http://www.csis.org/media/csis/pubs/ttu_0406.pdf

Charters, D., & Walker, G. (2002/2003) *After 9/11: Terrorism and crime in a globalized world.* Utrecht: Centre for Conflict Studies. Retrieved from http://centreforforeignpolicystudies.dal.ca/pdf/AFTER911toc.pdf

Cheney, R. (2002, June 6). *Remarks to the National Association of Home Builders.* Washington, DC. Retrieved from http://www.whitehouse.gov/vicepresident/newsspeeches/speeches/vp20020606.html

Chipman, J. (2004). *The military balance 2003–2004*. London: Oxford University Press (for the International Institute for Strategic Studies).

Clausewitz, C. V. (1976). *On war* (M. Howard & P. Paret, Eds. and trans.). Princeton, NJ: Princeton University Press.

CNN Inside Politics. (2002, August 16). *Some Republicans question Bush strategy*. Retrieved from http://archives.cnn.com/2002/ALLPOLITICS/08/16/bush.iraq/

CNN Television. (2002, September 8). *Search for the smoking gun*. Interview of Condoleezza Rice by Wolf Blitzer.

Conetta, C. (2003, October 20). *The wages of war: Iraqi combatant and noncombatant fatalities in the 2003 conflict*. Project on Defense Alternatives, Research Monograph No. 8. Retrieved from http://www.comw.org/pda/0310rm8.html

Cook, T. D., & Campbell, D. T. (1979). In T. D. Cook and D. T. Campbell (Eds.), Quasi-experiments: Interrupted time-series designs. In *Quasi experimentation: Design and analysis for field settings* (pp. 207–232). Boston: Houghton Mifflin.

Cordesman, A. (2004, December 22). *The developing Iraqi insurgency: Status at end-2004*. CSIS Working Draft. Retrieved from http://www.CSIS.org

Cortright, D. (2000, May 2). *Positive inducements in international statecraft*. Paper prepared for the conference on Promoting Human Rights: Isolation or Investment, sponsored by the Fraser Institute, Calgary, Canada. Retrieved from http://www.fourthfreedom.org/Applications/cms.php?page_id=39

Cortright, D., Millar, A., Lopez, G. A., & Gerbe, L. M. (2003, November). *Toward a more secure America: Grounding U.S. policy in global realities*. Joan B. Kroc Institute for International Peace Studies and Fourth Freedom Forum. Retrieved from http://www.secureamerica.us/pdf/sa_report.pdf

Crenshaw, M. (1981). The causes of terrorism. *Comparative Politics, 13*(4), 379–399.

Crenshaw, M. (1991). How terrorism declines. In C. McCauley (Ed.), *Terrorism, research and public policy* (pp. 69–87). London: Frank Cass.

Cronin, A.K. (2002). Rethinking sovereignty: American strategy in the age of terrorism. *Survival, 44*(2), 119–139.

Cronin, A.K. (2002/2003). Behind the curve: Globalization and international terrorism. *International Security, 27*(3), 30–58.

Cunningham, W. G. (2002, November). Terrorism definitions and typologies. In R. S. Moore (Ed.), *Terrorism: Concepts, causes and conflict resolution* (pp. 5–40). Fort Belvoir, VA: Advanced Systems and Concepts Office, Defense Threat Reduction

Agency and Working Group on War, Violence and Terrorism, Institute for Conflict Analysis and Resolution, George Mason University.

De Wijk, R. (2002). The limits of military power. *Washington Quarterly, 25*(1), 75–92.

Dekmejian, R. H. (1995). *Islam in revolution: Fundamentalism in the Arab world* (2nd ed.). Syracuse, NY: Syracuse University Press.

Della Porta, D. (1996). Social movements and the state: Thoughts on the policing of protest. In D. McAdam, J. D. McCarthy, & M. N. Zald (Eds.), *Comparative perspectives on social movement* (pp. 62–92). Cambridge, U.K.: Cambridge University Press.

Dershowitz, A. (2002). *Why terrorism works: Understanding the threat, responding to the challenge.* New Haven, CT: Yale University Press.

Deutsch, M. (1973). *The resolution of conflict.* New Haven, CT: Yale University Press.

Druckman, D. (1986). Stages, turning points and crises: Negotiating military base rights, Spain and the United States. *Journal of Conflict Resolution, 30*, 327–360.

Druckman, D. (1998). Social exchange theory: Premises and prospects. *International Negotiation Journal, 3*(2) 253–266.

Druckman, D. (2005). *Doing research: Methods of inquiry for conflict analysis.* Thousand Oaks, CA: Sage.

Druckman, D., & Green, J. (1986). *Political stability in the Philippines: Framework and analysis.* Monograph Series in World Affairs No. 22(3). Denver, CO: University of Denver.

Druckman, D., Husbands, J. L., & Johnson, K. (1991). Dimensions of international negotiation. *Negotiation Journal, 7*, 89–108.

Duffield, M. (2002). War as network enterprise: The new security terrain and its implications. *Cultural Values, 6*(1/2), 153–165.

Enders, W., & Sandler, T. (1990). UN conventions, technology and retaliation in the fight against terrorism: An econometric evaluation. *Terrorism and Political Violence, 2*(1), 83–105.

Enders, W., & Sandler, T. (1992). A time-series analysis of transnational terrorism: Trends and cycles. *Defense Economics, 3*(4), 305–320.

Enders, W., & Sandler, T. (1993). The effectiveness of anti-terrorism policies: Vector-autoregression-intervention analysis. *American Political Science Review, 87*(4), 829–844.

Enders, W., & Sandler, T. (1996). Terrorism and foreign direct investment in Spain and Greece. *Kyklos, 49,* 331–352.

Enders, W., & Sandler, T. (2000). Is transnational terrorism becoming more threatening? A time-series investigation. *Journal of Conflict Resolution, 44*(3), 307–332.

Enders, W., & Sandler, T. (2002). Patterns of transnational terrorism, 1979–1999. *International Studies Quarterly, 46,* 145–165.

Enders, W., & Sandler, T. (2004). What do we know about the substitution effect in transnational terrorism? In A. Silke & G. Ilardi (Eds.), *Researching terrorism trends, achievements, failures.* London: Frank Cass 119–137.

Enders, W., & Sandler, T. (2005). After 9/11: Is it all different now? *Journal of Conflict Resolution, 49*(2), 259–277.

Enders, W., Sandler, T., & Cauley, J. (1990). Assessing the impact of terrorism-thwarting policies: An intervention times series approach. *Defense Economics, 2*(1), 1–18.

Enders, W., Sandler, T., & Parise, G. F. (1992). An econometric analysis of the impact of terrorism on tourism. *Kyklos, 45,* 531–554.

Erlanger, S. (2001, September 27). Berlusconi vaunts West's superiority. *International Herald Tribune.* Retrieved from Global Policy Forum http://www .globalpolicy.org/wtc/analysis/0927berlu.htm

Erlanger, S. (2006, January 26). Hamas Presses Fatah in Palestinian Vote, Surveys Say. *New York Times,* A1.

Esposito, J. L. (1995). *The Islamic threat: Myth or reality?* (2nd ed.). New York: Oxford University Press.

Esposito, J. L., & Voll, J. O. (1996). *Islam and democracy.* New York: Oxford University Press.

Falkenrath, R. A. (2000, October). *Analytic models and policy prescription: Understanding recent innovation in U.S. counter-terrorism.* BCSIA Discussion Paper 2000-31, ESDP Discussion Paper ESDP-2000-03. Boston: John F. Kennedy School of Government, Harvard University.

Faure, M. A. (1994). Some methodological problems in comparative politics. *Journal of Theoretical Politics, 6,* 307–322.

Fearon, J. D. (1995). Rationalist explanations for war. *International Organization, 49*(3), 379–414.

Fisher, R. (1969). *International conflict for beginners.* New York: Harper & Row.

Fleischer, A., & Buccola, S. (2002). War, terror, and the tourism market in Israel. *Applied Economics, 34*, 1335–1343.

Fowler, W. (1981). *Terrorism data bases: A comparison of missions, methods and systems* [Appendix]. Rand Note N-1503-RC. Santa Monica, CA: Rand Corporation.

Francisco, R. A. (2001, January 14–21). *The dictator's dilemma.* Paper prepared for the conference on Repression and Mobilization: What Do We Know and Where Do We Go From Here? University of Maryland. Retrieved from http://web .ku.edu/ronfran/dictatorsdilemma.htm#_ftn1

Franklin, E. W. (2004). Preemption and just war: Considering the case of Iraq. *Parameters, 34*(4), 20–39.

Frey, B. (2004). Decentralisation as a disincentve for terror. *European Journal of Political Economy, 20*, 509–515.

Gaddis, J. L. (2002). A grand strategy of transformation. *Foreign Policy, November/ December*, 50–57.

Gaddis, J. L. (2004). *Surprise, security, and the American experience.* Boston: Harvard University Press.

Gamson, W. A. (1975). *The strategy of social protest.* Homewood, AL: Dorsey Press.

George, A., & Bennett, A. (2005). Process tracing and historical explanation. In A. George & A. Bennett (Eds.), *Case studies and theory development in the social science* (pp. 205–232). Cambridge: MIT Press.

George, A., & Smoke, R. (1974). *Deterrence in American foreign policy: Theory and practice.* New York: Columbia University Press.

Glaser, S. B. (2005a, May 1). Global terrorism statistics debated: New report leaves some wondering how to measure the number of attacks. *Washington Post*, p. A023.

Glaser, S. B. (2005b, April 28). Global terrorism statistics released: Clearinghouse data show sharp rise. *Washington Post*, p. A07.

Glaser, S. B. (2005c, April 27). U.S. figures show sharp global rise in terrorism: State Dept. will not put data in report. *Washington Post*, p. A01.

Goldstone, J. A., & Tilly, C. (2001). Opportunity (and threat): Popular action and state response in the dynamics of contentious action. In R. A. Amizade, D. McAdam, E. Perry, S. Tarrow, & C. Tilly (Eds.), *Silence and voice in the study of contentious politics* (pp. 179–194). Cambridge, U.K.: Cambridge University Press.

Gorman, C., Robinson, S., & Walsh, B. (2005, November 2).The bills take on the summit: Humanitarian aid as smart politics. *Time*. Retrieved from *Time Online* http://time.blogs.com/global_health/2005/11/the_bills_take_.html

Greene, T. H. (1984). *Comparative revolutionary movements*. Englewood Cliffs, NJ: Prentice Hall.

Grier, P. (2004, December 17). The rising tab for U.S. war effort. *Christian Science Monitor*. Retrieved from http://www.csmonitor.com/2004/1217/p01s01-usmi.html

Gunaratna, R. (2002). *Inside Al Qaeda: Global network of terror*. New York: Berkeley Books.

Gunaratna, R. (2004). The post-Madrid face of Al-Qaeda. *Washington Quarterly, 27*(3), 91–100.

Gurr, T. R. (1970). *Why men rebel*. Princeton, NJ: Princeton University Press.

Gurr, T. R., & Goldstone, J. (1991). Comparisons and policy implications. In J. Goldstone, T. R. Gurr, & F. Moshiri (Eds.), *Revolutions in the late twentieth century*. Boulder, CO: Westview Press, 324–352.

Haddad, Y. (1992). Islamists and the "problem of Israel": The 1967 awakening. *Middle East Journal, 46*(2), 266–285.

Hafez, M. M., & Wiktorowicz, Q. (2004). Violence as contention in the Islamic Egyptian movement. In Q. Wiktorowicz (Ed.), *Islamic activism: A social movement theory approach* (pp. 61–88). Bloomington: Indiana University Press.

Hamilton, L. C., & Hamilton, J. D. (1983). Dynamics of terrorism. *International Studies Quarterly, 27*, 39–54.

Hanley, C. (2004, September 26). War deaths said to be declining. *Washington Times*. Retrieved from http://washingtontimes.com/world/20040926-103900-9842r.htm

Harkabi, Y. (1990). *War and strategy* (Hebrew). Tel Aviv: Israel Ministry of Defense.

Hartung, W. (2003, February 19). *The hidden costs of war*. Fourth Freedom Organization. Retrieved from http://www.iansa.org/iraq/hidden_costs.htm

Harvey, F. (Spring 1997). "Deterrence and Ethnic Conflict: The Case of Bosnia-Herzogovina, 1993–94." *Security Studies, 6*(3), 185.

Hocke, P. (1999). Determining the selection bias in local and national newspaper reports on protest events. In D. Rucht, R. Koopmans, & F. Niedhardt (Eds.), *Acts of dissent: New developments in the study of protest.* Lanham, MD: Rowman & Littlefield, 131–163.

Hoffman, B. (1998). *Inside terrorism.* New York: Columbia University Press.

Hoffman, B. (2003). Defining terrorism. In R. D. Howard & R. L. Sawyer (Eds.), *Terrorism and counter-terrorism: Understanding the new security environment.* Guilford, CT: McGraw-Hill/Dushkin.

Holmes, K. R. (2005, July 26). What's in a name? "War on terror" out, "struggle against extremism." Web Memo No. 805. Heritage Foundation. Retrieved from http://www.heritage.org

Horne, A. (1977). *A savage war of peace: Algeria, 1954–1962.* New York: Penguin.

Huntington, S. P. (1993, Summer). The clash of civilizations. *Foreign Affairs, 72*(3), 22–28.

Iannaccone, L. R. (2003). The market for martyrs. Presented at the 2004 Meetings of the American Economic Association, San Diego, CA.

Ibrahim, S. E. (1980). Anatomy of Egypt's militant groups. *International Journal of Middle East Studies, 12*(4), 423–453.

International Institute for Strategic Studies. (2003). *Strategic Survey 2002/2003, An evaluation and forecast of world affairs.* London: Oxford University Press.

Jenkins, B. (2002). *Countering al-Qaeda: An appreciation of the situation and suggestions for strategy.* RAND Publication No. 15. Retrieved from http://www.rand.org/publications/MR/MR1620/

Jentleson, B. W. (2002). The need for praxis: Bringing policy relevance back in. *International Security, 26*(4), 169–183.

Jervis, R. (1979) "Deterrence Theory Revisited." *World Politics, 32*(2), 289–324.

Jervis, R. L. (2003). The confrontation between Iraq and the U.S.: Implications for the theory and practice of deterrence. *European Journal of International Relations, 9*(2), 315–337.

Juergensmeyer, M. (2003). *Terror in the mind of God: The global rise of religious violence.* Berkeley: University of California Press.

Karklins, R., & Peterson, R. (1989). Decision calculus of protesters and regimes: Eastern Europe. *Journal of Politics, 555*(3), 321–341.

Kegley, C. W. (Ed.). (1990). *International terrorism: Characteristics, causes, controls.* New York: St. Martin's Press.

Kegley, C. W. (Ed.). (2003). *The new global terrorism.* Englewood Cliffs, NJ: Prentice Hall.

Kepel, G. (1993). *Muslim extremism in Egypt: The Prophet and the Pharaoh.* Berkeley: University of California Press.

Kiras, J. D. (2002). Terrorism and irregular warfare. In J. Baylis, J. Wirtz, E. Cohen, & C. S. Gray (Eds.), *Strategy in the contemporary world, An introduction to strategic studies* (pp. 208–232). New York: Oxford University Press.

Kiser, S. (2004). *Financing terror: An analysis and simulation to affect Al Qaeda's financial infrastructures.* PhD dissertation, RAND Pardee Graduate School. Retrieved from http://www.rand.org/pubs/rgs_dissertations/RGSD185/

Koopman, R., & Rucht, D. (2002). Protest event analysis. In K. Bert & S. Staggenborg (Eds.), *Methods of social movement research* (pp. 231–259). Minneapolis: University of Minnesota Press.

Krane, J. (2004, July 9). U.S. officials: Iraq insurgency bigger. *Philadelphia Inquirer*, p. z004.

Kriesberg, L. (1998). *Constructive conflicts: From escalation to resolution.* Oxford: Rowman & Littlefield.

Krueger, A. (2003, May 29). Poverty doesn't create terrorists. *New York Times*, p. C2.

Krueger, A., & Laitin, D. (2004). "Misunderestimating" terrorism. *Foreign Affairs, 83*(5), 8–13.

Krueger, A. B., & Maleckova, J. (2003a, June 6). Seeking the roots of terror. *Chronicle of Higher Education*, p. B10. Retrieved from http://chronicle.com/free/v49/i39/39b01001.htm

Krueger, A. B., & Maleckova, J. (2003b). Education, poverty and terrorism: Is there a causal connection? *Journal of Economic Perspectives, 17*(4), 119–144.

Lacina, B., Russett, B., & Gleditsch, N. P. (2005). *The declining risk of death in battle.* Paper presented at panel on Examining War Deaths I: How Many Soldiers and Civilians Die? 46th Annual ISA Convention, March 1–5, Honolulu, Hawaii.

Lai, B. (2003). *Examining the number of incidents of terrorism within states, 1968–1977.* Paper presented at the American Political Science Association Meeting, Philadelphia, PA.

Lai, B. (2004). *Explaining terrorism using the framework of opportunity and willingness: An empirical examination of international terrorism.* Paper presented at the Political Science Workshop Series, April 23, University of Iowa.

Lake, D. (2002). Rational extremism: Understanding terrorism in the twenty-first century. *Dialogue-IO, Spring*, 15–29.

Lake, D. (2003). International relations theory and internal conflict: Insights from the interstices. *International Studies Review, 5*(4), 81–89.

Langhor, V. (2001). Of Islamists and ballot boxes: Rethinking the relationship between Islamists and electoral politics. *International Journal of Middle East Studies, November*, 591–610.

Laqueur, W. (1977). *Terrorism*. Boston: Little, Brown.

Laqueur, W. (1987). *The age of terrorism*. Boston: Little, Brown.

Laqueur, W. (1999). *The new terrorism: Fanaticism and the arms of mass destruction*. New York: Oxford University Press.

Lewis, B. (2003). *The crisis of Islam: Holy war and unholy terror*. New York: Random House.

Lichbach, M. I. (1987). Deterrence or escalation? The puzzle of aggregate studies of repression and dissent. *Journal of Conflict Resolution, 31*(2), 266–297.

Lichbach, M. I. (2005). Information, trust and power: The impact of conflict histories, policy regimes, and political institutions on terrorism. *International Studies Review, 7*(1), 162–165.

Lohmann, S. (1994). The dynamics of informational cascades: The Monday demonstrations in Leipzig, East Germany, 1989–1991. *World Politics, 47*(1), 42–101.

Lynch, C. (2002, December 19). Volunteers swell a reviving Qaeda, UN warns. *International Herald Tribune*, p. 3.

Machiavelli, N. (1998). *The prince*. Cambridge, U.K.: Cambridge University Press.

Mack, A. J. R. (1975). Why big nations lose small wars: The politics of asymmetric conflict. *World Politics, 27*(2), 175–200.

Malik, O. (2001). *Enough of the definition of terrorism!* London: Royal Institute of International Affairs.

Malvesti, M. L. (2001). Explaining the United States' decision to strike back at terrorists. *Terrorism and Political Violence, 13*(2), 85–100.

Manning, W. G. (1998). The logged dependent variable, heteroscedasticity, and the retransformation problem. *Journal of Health Economics, 17*(3), 283–295.

Mao, T.T. (1961). *On guerilla warfare* (S. B. Griffith, trans.). New York: Praeger.

Mao, T.T. (1966). *Selected military writings of Mao Tse-Tung*. Peking: Foreign Language Press.

Maoz, Z. (1990). *Paradoxes of war: On the art of national self-entrapment*. Boston: Unwin Hyman.

Marighella, C. (1985). *The terrorist classic: Manual of the urban guerilla* (G. Hanrahan, trans.). Chapel Hill, NC: Documentary Publications.

Marshall, M. G. (2002, September 11). *Global terrorism: An overview and analysis*. Center for International Development and Conflict Management (CIDCM), University of Maryland, College Park.

Martinez-Herrera, E. (2003). *Public order policies, responsive policies, terrorism and nationalist extremist in the Basque country*. Paper presented at ECPR Joint Session, Workshop 4, Defending Democracy, March 29–April 4, Edinburgh, Scotland. Retrieved from http://www.essex.ac.uk/ecpr/events/jointsessions/paperarchive/edinburgh/ws4/MartinezHerrera.pdf

Mason, T. D., & Krane, D. A. (1989). The political economy of death squads: Toward a theory of the impact of state-sanctioned terror. *International Studies Quarterly, 33*(2), 175–198.

McAdam, D. (1982). *Political process and the development of black insurgency, 1930–1970*. Chicago: University of Chicago Press.

McAdam, D. (1983). Tactical innovation and the pace of insurgency. *American Sociological Review, 48*, 735–754.

McCarthy, J. D., & Zald, M. N. (1977). Resource mobilization and social movements: A partial theory. *American Journal of Sociology, 82*, 1212–1241.

McCarthy, R. (2004, December 16). For faith and country: Insurgents fight on. *The Guardian*. Retrieved from http://www.guardian.co.uk/Iraq/Story/0,2763,1374632,00.html

McCauley, C. (1991). Terrorism, research and public policy: An overview. In C. McCauley (Ed.), *Terrorism research and public policy* (pp. 133–134). London: Frank Cass.

McDowall, D., McCleary, R., Meidinger, E., & Hay, R. A. (1980). *Interrupted time series analysis*. Sage University Paper Series on Quantitative Applications in the Social Sciences, No. 07-021. Beverly Hills, CA: Sage.

McGlinchey, E. (2004). *Constructing militant opposition: Authoritarian rule and militant Islam in Central Asia*. Paper presented at the Central Asia and the Caucasus in a Globalized World Lecture Series, April 6, Yale University, New Haven, CT. Retrieved from http://www.yale.edu/ycias/centralasia/mcglin_yale.pdf

McLemee, S. (2002, September 23). 100 Christian ethicists challenge claim that preemptive war on Iraq would be morally justified. *Chronicle of Higher Education* [Web Daily]. Retrieved from http://maxspeak.org/gm/archives/chron.htm

McNamara, R. (1995, April 25). *In retrospect—The tragedy and lessons of Vietnam.* New York: Vintage Books, Random House, Inc.) pp. 127–319.

McPhail, C., & Schweingruber, D. (1999). Unpacking protest events: A description bias analysis of media records with systematic direct observation of collective action—The 1995 March for Life in Washington, DC. In D. Rucht, R. Koopmans, & F. Niedhardt (Eds.), *Acts of dissent: New developments in the study of protest* (pp. 164–198). Boulder, CO: Rowman & Littlefield.

Mearsheimer, J. J., & Walt, S. M. (2005). An unnecessary war. *Foreign Policy, January/February,* 51–59.

Merari, A. (1993). Terrorism as a strategy of insurgency. *Terrorism and Political Violence, 5*(4), 213–251.

Mickolus, E. F. (1980). *Transnational terrorism: A chronology of events, 1968–1979.* Westport, CT: Greenwood Press.

Mickolus, E. F. (1982). *International terrorism: Attributes of terrorist events, 1968–1977, ITERATE 2 Data Codebook.* Ann Arbor, MI: Inter-University Consortium for Political and Social Research.

Mickolus, E. F. (1987). Terrorists, governments, and numbers: Counting things versus things that count. *Journal of Conflict Resolution, 31*(1), 54–62.

Mickolus, E. F. (1993). Terrorism, 1988–1991: A chronology of events and a selectively annotated bibliography, bibliographies and indexes. In *Military studies,* No. 6. Westport, CT: Greenwood Press.

Mickolus, E. F. (2002). How do we know we're winning the war against terrorists? Issues in measurement. *Studies in Conflict & Terrorism, 25,* 151–160.

Mickolus, E. F., & Flemming, P. (1988). *Terrorism, 1980–1987: A selectively annotated bibliography.* Westport, CT: Greenwood Press.

Mickolus, E. F., Sandler, T., & Murdock, J. (1989). *International terrorism in the 1980s: A chronology, Volume 2: 1984–1987.* Ames: Iowa State University Press.

Mickolus, E. F., Sandler, T., Murdock, J., & Fleming, P. (2003). *International terrorism: Attributes of terrorist events, 1968–2002, ITERATE Data Codebook.* Retrieved from http://ssdc.ucsd.edu/ssdc/pdf/ITERATECodebook2003.pdf

Mickolus, E. F., & Simmons, S. L. (1997). *Terrorism, 1992–1995: A chronology of events and a selectively annotated bibliography*. Westport, CT: Greenwood Press.

Mickolus, E. F., & Simmons, S. L. (2002). *Terrorism, 1996–2001: A chronology of events and a selectively annotated bibliography* (2 vols.). Westport, CT: Greenwood Press.

Midlarsky, M. I., Crenshaw, M., & Yoshida, F. (1980). Why violence spreads: The contagion of international terrorism. *International Studies Quarterly, 24*(2), 262–298.

Ministry of Home Affairs, Republic of Singapore. (2003, January 7). *White paper– The Jemaah Islamiyah arrests and the threat of terrorism.*

MIPT National Memorial Institute for the Prevention of Terrorism. (2002). "Understanding the terrorism database." *MIPT Quarterly Bulletin*: 4–6.

MIPT Oklahoma City National Memorial Institute for the Prevention of Terrorism. *Rand-MIPT Terrorism Incident Database*. Retrieved from http://www.tkb.org/

Mooradian, M., & Druckman, D. (1999). Hurting stalemate or mediation? The conflict over Nagorno-Karabakh, 1990–95. *Journal of Peace Research, 36*(6), 709–727.

Morgan, P. M. (1977). *Deterrence: A conceptual analysis.* London: Sage.

Munson, Z. (2001). Islamic mobilization: Social movement theory and the Egyptian Muslim Brotherhood. *Sociological Quarterly, 42*(4), 487–510.

National Foreign Assessment Center, Central Intelligence Agency. (1978). *International terrorism in 1977: A research paper.* Washington, DC: Author [RP 78 102554, 1978, 1].

National War College. (2002, May). *Combating terrorism in a globalized world.* Retrieved from http://www.au.af.mil/au/awc/awcgate/ndu/n02combating_terrorism.pdf

Nelson, P. S., & Scot, J. L. (1992). Terrorism and the media: An empirical analysis. *Defense Economics, 2,* 329–339.

Neter, J., Wasserman, W., & Whitmore, G. (Eds.). (1988). Times series and forecasting I: Classical methods. In *Applied statistics* (3rd ed.). Boston: Allyn & Bacon.

Nitsch, V., & Schumacher, D. (2004). Terrorism and international trade: An empirical investigation. *European Journal of Political Economy, 20*(2), 423–433.

Nye, J. S. (2001). *The paradox of American power: Why the world's only superpower can't go it alone.* New York: Oxford University Press.

Nye, J. S. (2004). *Soft power: The means to success in world politics.* New York: Public Affairs.

Obaid, N., & Cordesman, A. (2005, September 19). *Saudi militants in Iraq: assessment and Kingdom's response.* CSIS. Retrieved from http://www.csis.org/index .php?option=com_csis_pubs&task=view&id=1442

O'Brien, S. (1996). Foreign policy crises and the resort to terrorism: A time series analysis of conflict linkages. *Journal of Conflict Resolution, 40*(2), 320–335.

O'Hanlon, M. E., Rice, S. E., & Steinberg, J. B. (2002, December). *The new national security strategy and preemption.* Brookings Institution Policy Brief. Washington, DC: Brookings Institution.

Oots, K. L. (1986). *A political organization approach to transnational terrorism.* Westport, CT: Greenwood.

Opotow, S. (2000). Aggression and violence. In M. Deutsch & P. Coleman (Eds.), *The handbook of conflict resolution: Theory and practice.* San Francisco: Jossey-Bass, pp. 403–427.

Opp, K.-D., & Roehl, W. (1990). Repression, micromobilization, and political protest. *Social Forces, 69*, 521–547.

Overgaard, P. B. (1994). The scale of terrorist attacks as a signal of resources. *Journal of Conflict Resolution, 38*(3), 452–478.

Paden, J. N. (2005). *Muslim civic cultures and conflict resolution: The challenge of democratic federalism in Nigeria.* Washington, DC: Brookings Institution Press.

Paden, J. N., & Singer, P. W. (2003). America slams the door (on its foot): Washington's destructive new visa policies. *Foreign Affairs, 82*(3), 8–14.

Pankratz, A. (1991). *Forecasting with dynamic regression models.* New York: John Wiley.

Pape, R. A. (1996). *Bombing to win: Air power and coercion in war.* Ithaca, NY: Cornell University Press.

Pape, R. (2002). The strategic logic of suicide terrorism. *American Political Science Review, 97*(3), 343–361.

Pape, R. (2005). *Dying to win: The strategic logic of suicide terrorism.* New York: Random House.

Parks, C., & Komorita, S. S. (1998). Reciprocity research and its implications for the negotiation process. *International Negotiation Journal, 3*(2), 151–169.

Parsa, M. (1989). *Social origins of the Iranian Revolution.* New Brunswick, NJ: Rutgers University Press.

Patchen, M. (1987). Strategies for eliciting cooperation from an adversary: Laboratory and international findings. *Journal of Conflict Resolution, 31*(1), 164–185.

Patchen, M. (1998a). *Resolving disputes between nations: Coercion or conciliation?* Durham, NC: Duke University Press.

Patchen, M. (1998b). When does reciprocity in the actions of nations occur? *International Negotiation Journal, 3*(2), 171–196.

Perito, R. (2003). *Where is the lone ranger when we need him: America's quest for a post conflict stability force.* Washington, DC: United States Institute of Peace Press.

Peters, R. (2003, March 23). Revolutionizing warfare on the fly. *Atlanta Journal—Constitution,* D6.

Peters, R. (2004). In praise of attrition. *Parameters, Summer,* 24–32.

Pew Research Center for the People and the Press. (2003, June 3). *Views of a changing world: War with Iraq further divides global publics.* Retrieved from http://people-press.org/reports/display.php3?ReportID=185

Pew Research Center for the People and the Press. (2004, March 16). *A year after Iraq war: Mistrust of America in Europe ever higher, Muslim anger persists.* Retrieved from http://people-press.org/reports/display.php3?ReportID=206

Pillar, P. (2004). "Counter-terrorism after Al Qaeda." *Washington Quarterly, 27, 101–114.*

Pincus, W., & Priest, D. (2003, May 6). Spy agencies optimism on Al Qaeda is growing: Lack of attacks thought to show group is nearly crippled. *Washington Post,* p. A16.

Pion-Berlin, D. (1984). The political economy of state repression in Argentina. In M. Stohl & G. A. Lopez (Eds.), *State as terrorist: The dynamics of governmental violence and repression* (pp. 99–122). Westport, CT: Greenwood Press.

Popper, K. R. (1972). *Objective knowledge: An evolutionary approach.* Oxford: Oxford University Press.

Posen, B. R. (2001/2002). The struggle against terrorism: Grand strategy, strategy, and tactics. *International Security, 26*(3), 39–55.

Prestowitz, C. (2003). *Rogue nation: American unilateralism and the failure of good intentions.* New York: Basic Books.

Pruitt, D., & Rubin, J. (1986). *Social conflicts.* New York: Random House.

Public Broadcasting Service. Frontline. *Timeline Al Qaeda's global context.* Retrieved from http://www.pbs.org/wgbh/pages/frontline/shows/knew/etc/cron.html

Putnam, R. D. (1993). *Making democracy work: Civic traditions in modern Italy.* Princeton, NJ: Princeton University Press.

RAND Terrorism Database Project. *Understanding the terrorism database.* Retrieved from http://www.rand.org/ise/projects/terrorismdatabase/index.html

Rasler, K. (1996). Concessions, repression and political protest in the Iranian Revolution. *American Sociological Review, 61,* 132–152.

Record, J. (2003, December). *Bounding the global war on terrorism.* Strategic Studies Institute, U.S. Army War College. Retrieved from http://www.globalsecurity.org/military/library/report/2003/record_bounding.pdf

Reich, W. (Ed.). (1998). *Origins of terrorism: Psychologies, ideologies, theologies, states of mind.* Washington, DC: Woodrow Wilson Center Press.

Reiter, D. (2003). Exploring the bargaining model of war. *Perspectives on Politics, 1*(1), 27–43.

Rice, C. (2005, January 19). *Remarks in transcript 2nd day of Rice hearings.* Federal News Service. Retrieved from http://www.brainthink.com/view_article.php?articleid = 2052

Roberts, B. (1998). NBC-armed rogues: Is there a moral case for preemption? In E. Abrams (Ed.), *Close calls, intervention, terrorism, missile defense and "just war" today.* Washington, DC: Ethics and Public Policy Center 83–107.

Roberts, L., Lafta, R., Garfield, R., Khudhairi, J., & Burnham, G. (2004). Mortality before and after the 2003 invasion of Iraq: Cluster sample survey. *Lancet, 364,* 1857–1864.

Robinson, G. (2003). The Palestinian "Intifada" revolt. In J. Goldstone (Ed.), *Revolutions: Theoretical, comparative and historical studies* (pp. 304–310, 3rd ed.). Stamford, CT: Thomson-Wadsworth.

Robinson, G. (2004). Hamas as social movement. In Q. Wiktorowicz (Ed.), *Islamic activism: A social movement theory approach* (pp. 112–142). Indianapolis: Indiana University Press.

Robson, C. (2002). *Real world research: A resource for social scientists and practitioner-researchers* (2nd ed.). Malden, MA: Blackwell.

Rock, S. M. (1995). Impact of the 65 mph speed limit on accidents, deaths, and injuries in Illinois. *Accident Analysis and Prevention, 27*(2), 207–214.

Rosendorff, P., & Sandler, T. (2004). Too much of a good thing: The proactive response dilemma. *Journal of Conflict Resolution, 48*(5), 657–671.

Rosendorff, P., & Sandler, T. (2005). The political economy of transnational terrorism. *Journal of Conflict Resolution, 49*(2), 171–671.

Rubenstein, R. (2003). The psycho-political sources of terrorism. In C. Kegley (Ed.), *The new global terrorism* (pp. 139–150). Englewood Cliffs, NJ: Prentice Hall.

Rubin, J., Pruitt, D., & Kim, S. H. (1986). *Social conflict: Escalation, stalemate and settlement.* New York: Random House.

Rumsfeld, D. (2001, September 27). A new kind of war. *New York Times.*

Rumsfeld, D. (2003, October 16). Memo. Retrieved from http://www.globalsecurity .org/military/library/policy/dod/rumsfeld-d20031016sdmemo.htm

Rumsfeld, D. (2005, December 12). *Remarks from "Transcript: Secretary of Defense Donald Rumsfeld's speech on the future of Iraq."* Delivered at the Johns Hopkins School of Advanced International Studies, December 5, 2005. *Washington Post.* Retrieved from http://www.washingtonpost.com/wp-dyn/content/ article/2005/12/05/AR2005120501248.html

Saleh, B. (2004). *Economic conditions and resistance to occupation in the West Bank and Gaza Strip: There is a causal connection. Topics in Middle Eastern and North African Economics,* 6. Retrieved from online journal http://www.luc .edu/orgs/meea/volume6/meea6.htm

Sandler, T. (2003).Collective action and transnational terrorism. *World Economy, 26*(6), 779–802.

Sandler, T., & Enders, W. (2004). An economic perspective on transnational terrorism. *European Journal of Political Economy, 20*, 301–316.

Sandler, T., & Lapan, H. E. (1988). The calculus of dissent: An analysis of terrorists' choice of targets. *Synthese, 76*(2), 245–261.

Sandler, T., Tschirhart, J. T., & Cauley, J. (1983). A theoretical analysis of transnational terrorism. *American Political Science Review, 77*(1), 36–54.

Sandole, D. J. D. (1993). Paradigms, theories, and metaphors in conflict and conflict resolution: Coherence or confusion? In D. J. D. Sandole & H. van der Merwe

(Eds.), *Conflict resolution theory and practice: Integration and application.* Manchester, U.K.: Manchester University Press 3–24.

Sandole, D. J. D. (1998). A comprehensive mapping of conflict and conflict resolution: A three pillar approach. *Peace and Conflict Studies, 5*(2), 1–30.

Sandole, D. J. D. (1999). *Capturing the complexity of conflict: Dealing with violent ethnic conflicts of the post-Cold War era.* London: Frances Pinter.

Sandole, D. J. D. (2002, November). The causes of terrorism. In *Terrorism, concepts, causes, and conflict resolution,* Advanced Systems and Concepts Office, Defense Threat Reduction Agency, and ICAR Working Group on War, Violence and Terrorism, Institute for Conflict Analysis and Resolution, George Mason University, Fort Belvoir, Virginia, pp. 88–119.

Sandole, D. J. D. (2005). *The Islamic-Western "clash of civilizations": The inadvertent contribution of the Bush presidency.* Paper presented at the annual meeting of the International Studies Association (ISA), March 1–5, Honolulu, Hawaii. Retrieved from http://www.isanet.org

Sanger, D. (2003, May 2). President says military phase in Iraq has ended. *New York Times*, p. 1.

SAS/ETS users guide. (1999). *Intervention models and interrupted time series.* Retrieved from http://www.uwm.edu/IMT/Computing/sasdoc8/sashtml/ets/chap7/sect13.htm

Schelling, T. C. (1963). *The strategy of conflict.* New York: Oxford University Press.

Schelling, T. C. (1996). *Arms and influence.* New Haven, CT: Yale University Press.

Schmid, A. P., & Jongman, A. J. (1988). *Political terrorism: A new guide to actors, authors, concepts, data bases, theories, and literature.* New Brunswick, NJ: Transaction Books.

Schmitt, E., & Shanker, T. (2005, July 2005). Washington recasts terror war as "struggle." *New York Times*, p. A1.

Schroeder, P. (2002). Iraq: "The case against preemptive war." *American Conservative, 21*(2), 8–20.

Scott, J. L. (2001). Media congestion limits media terrorism. *Defense and Peace Economics, 12,* 215–227.

Scowcroft, B. (2002, August 15). Don't attack Saddam. *Wall Street Journal.* Retrieved from http://www.opinionjournal.com/editorial/feature.html?id=110002133

Senechal de la Roche, R. (1996). Collective violence as social control. *Sociological Forum, 11*, 97–128.

Senechal de la Roche, R. (2004). Toward a scientific theory of terrorism. *Sociological Theory, 22*(1), 1–4.

Shambaugh, G., & Josiger, W. (2004). *Public prudence and its support for counterterrorism initiatives.* Paper presented at annual meeting of the American Political Science Association, Chicago, IL September 4 .

Shapiro, J., & Siegel, D. (2005). *Underfunding in terrorist organizations.* Paper presented at the annual meeting of the American Political Science Association, September 1, Washington, DC. Retrieved from http://www.allacademic.com/meta/p42207_index.html

Singer, P. W. (2004). The war on terrorism: The big picture. *Parameters, Summer,* 141–148.

Slim, H. (1998). *International humanitarianism's engagement with civil war in the 1990s: A glance at evolving practice and theory.* Briefing Paper for ActionAid, U.K. Retrieved from http://www.jha.ac//articles/a033.htm

Sprinzak, E. (1991). The process of delegitimization: Towards a linkage theory of political terrorism. In C. McCauley (Ed.), *Terrorism research and public policy* (pp. 50–68). London: Frank Cass.

StatSoft Electronic Textbook 1984–2003. *Interrupted time series ARIMA.* Retrieved from http://www.statsoft.com/textbook/sttimser.html#ageneral

Stern, J. (2003). *Terror in the name of god: Why religious militants kill.* New York: HarperCollins.

Stern, P., & Druckman, D. (2000). Evaluating interventions in history: The case of international conflict resolution. In P. Stern & D. Druckman (Eds.), *International conflict resolution after the Cold War* (pp. 38–89). Washington, DC: National Academy Press.

Stevenson, R. W. (2005, August 4). President makes it clear: Phrase is "war on terror." *New York Times*, p. 12.

Syed, A. Z. (2005, June 29). Why the West must engage Islamists. *International Herald Tribune.* Retrieved from http://www.iht.com/articles/2005/06/28/opinion/edsyed.php

Taber, R. (1965). *War of the flea: The classic study of guerrilla warfare.* New York: Lyle & Stuart.

Tibi, B. (1998). *The challenge of fundamentalism: Political Islam and the new world disorder.* Los Angeles: University of California Press.

Tilly, C. (1978). *From mobilization to revolution.* Reading, MA: Addison-Wesley.

Tilly, C. (2004). Terror, terrorism, terrorists. *Sociological Theory, 22*(1), 5–13.

Tovar, B. H. (1986). Thoughts on running a small war. *International Journal of Intelligence and Counterintelligence, 1*(3), 85–93.

Tufts University, The Fletcher School. (2004, October 2). *Extending the preemption debate: A reassessment of current theory and practice* [Panel Discussion]. Retrieved from http://fletcher.tufts.edu/news/2004/10/preemption.shtml

U.S. Agency for International Development (USAID). (2002). *Foreign aid in the national interest.* Washington, DC: Author.

U.S. Congressional Budget Office. (2003, September 3). *An analysis of the U.S. military's ability to sustain an occupation of Iraq* (pp. 3–7). Washington, DC: Author. Retrieved from http://www.cbo.gov/showdoc.cfm?index=4515& sequence = 0

U.S. Department of Defense. (2001, April). *Dictionary of military and associated terms.* Washington, DC: Author.

U.S. Department of State. (1996–2003). *Patterns of global terrorism* (Various Editions). Retrieved from http://www.state.gov/s/ct/rls/pgtrpt/2003

Van Dyke, N., & Soule, S. A. (2002). Structural social change and the mobilizing effect of threat: Explaining levels of patriot and militia organizing in the United States. *Social Problems, 49*(4), 497–520.

Reiss, T. (October 24, 2005). "The first conservative: How Peter Viereck inspired and lost a movement." *New Yorker,* Life and Letters. Retrieved from http://www.newyorker.com/archive/2005/10/24/051024fa_fact1

Walzer, M. (1977). *Just and unjust wars: A moral argument with historical illustrations.* New York: Basic Books.

Walzer, M. (2003, February 1). N-inspection yes, war no. *Daily Yomiuri.*

Weimann, G., & Bernd Brosius, H. (1988). The predictability of international terrorism: A time-series analysis. *Terrorism, 11,* 491–503.

Weisman, J. (2005, January 26). Record '05 deficit forecast: War costs to raise total to $427 billion. *Washington Post,* p. A01.

White House (September 2002). The National Security Strategy of the United States. Washington, DC.

White House (February 2003). The National Strategy for Combating Terrorism. Washington, DC.

White House. (2005, October 6). *President discusses war on terror at National Endowment for Democracy.* Washington, DC.

Wichern, D. W., & Jones, R. H. (1977). Assessing the impact of market disturbances using intervention analysis. *Management Science, 24,* 329–337.

Wickham, C. R. (1997). Islamic mobilization and political change: The Islamist trend in Egypt's professional associations. In J. Benin & J. Stork (Eds.), *Political Islam.* Berkeley: University of California Press, pp.120–135.

Wickham, C. R. (2002). *Mobilizing Islam: Religion, activism, and political change in Egypt.* New York: Columbia University Press.

Wiktorowicz, Q. (2001). *The management of Islamic activism: Salafis, the Muslim brotherhood and state power in Jordan,* Albany: State University of New York Press.

Wiktorowicz, Q. (Ed.). (2004). *Islamic activism: A social movement theory approach.* Indianapolis: Indiana University Press.

Wilkinson, P. (1986). *Terrorism and the liberal state* (2nd ed.). New York: New York University.

Willer, R. (2004). The effects of government-issued terror warnings on presidential approval ratings. *Current Research in Social Psychology, 10*(1). Retrieved from http://www.uiowa.edu/~grpproc/crisp/crisp.10.1.html

Woods, S. M. (2003). An analysis of bloody Sunday. *Online Journal of Peace and Conflict Resolution, 5*(1), 127–134. Retrieved from http://www.trinstitute.org/ojpcr/5_1woods.htm

Yin, R., & Newman, D. (1999). An intervention analysis of Hurricane Hugo's effect on South Carolina's stumpage prices. *Canadian Journal of Forestry Research, 29,* 779–787.

Yin, R. K. (1989). *Case study research: Design and methods.* Beverly Hills, CA: Sage.

Zakaria, F. (2005, November 14). Pssst…Nobody loves a torturer. *Newsweek,* p. 36.

Zimmerman, E. (1980). Macro-comparative research on political protest. In T. R. Gurr (Ed.), *Handbook of political conflict* (pp. 167–237). New York: Free Press.

Zwick, J. (1984). Militarism and repression in the Philippines. In M. Stohl & G. A. Lopez (Eds.), *The state as terrorist: The dynamics of governmental violence and repression.* Westport, CT: Greenwood Press.

INDEX

Author Index

About the Author

Ivan Sascha Sheehan is on the faculty of the Graduate Programs in Dispute Resolution at the University of Massachusetts Boston. He specializes in the current conflict between global terrorism and counterterrorism and is a frequent speaker on U.S. foreign policy in the Global War on Terror. Dr. Sheehan's research, based on terrorism incident data, examines the impact of preemptive force on terrorist activity and examines the implications for international conflict management. He earned his Ph.D. from George Mason University.

Professor Sheehan continues to serve as a Visiting Professor at the Institute for Conflict Analysis and Resolution where he teaches courses on international terrorism and counterterrorism. He previously taught in the International Studies Department at Bentley College.

Printed in the United States
204620BV00002B/10/A